The Layman's Guide
To Trading Stocks

Dave Landry

Stilwell & Company Publishing Group
Los Angeles, California

Published by Stilwell & Company Publishing Group, Los Angeles.
Distributed by Peterson/Manz Trading, Inc., Los Angeles

ISBN 978-0-9747653-3-4

To Marcy, in bull markets and in bear...

Preface

In early 2008, I was inspired to write this book after seeing a good friend needlessly lose a lot of money. Initially, it was only intended to change the way the average Joe thought about Wall Street. My goal was to help investors avoid the common pitfalls of following conventional wisdom and to protect them from counterproductive urges of human nature itself.

As the year progressed, I watched other friends and acquaintances buy "good companies," claim to be "in it for the long haul," increase position size because the market was "undervalued" or because a guru said that it had bottomed. What was worse, others simply followed trained professionals who assured them that "the market always goes up longer term."

As I watched more and more people lose money in one of the greatest bear markets in history, I felt compelled to add more and more information. The basic book that I had envisioned soon ballooned into much more. It dawned on me that in order for the average person to survive the markets they must learn to think more and more like a trader. What started out as a very basic beginner's book developed over two years into a complete guide for trading. If that makes you wonder whether this is an overly complicated text, you can put your concerns aside. My approach is a very simple one.

Even if you consider yourself a longer-term "investor," as you will soon see, it pays to think more like a trader. Doing this isn't difficult provided that you are willing to let go of your ego and let the market, and only the market, tell you what to do.

How to Use This Book

The amount of information I decided to cover here necessitated breaking this book into two sections. The first section assumes that you have very little or no trading knowledge. You are taking the first step to understand that conventional wisdom is wrong, charts lead the way, the trend is your friend, and that in order to make money, you must first not lose it. You will learn that you are your own worst enemy. Even if you are a seasoned trader, you will find this section useful. When you find yourself in a hole, the best thing to do is to head back to the basics.

Section two is for those wanting to take the next step. It contains patterns to help you get into trends early, how to scan for great stocks, and advanced discretionary techniques to help you beat the market by staying with winners while avoiding false moves, and minimizing damage on adverse moves.

INSPIRED BY THE LAYMAN
In January of 2008, the following conversation took place as I walked into church.

Usher: Hey Dave, what do you think of Apple?

Me: It's begun to drop from high levels and has been trending lower. Stocks overall are in trouble too. We could be in the early phases of a bear market.

Usher: It'll come back.

Since he's never asked me about a stock before he's owned it, I realize that anything else I would have said would have fallen on deaf ears. Therefore, I just smiled and took my seat.

A few days later, I received a panicky e-mail. Apple had continued to implode. My usher friend informed me that he was now down over 70 points on 500 shares—a loss of over $35,000. I felt bad for him, especially since there are very simple things that he could have done to avoid this loss. I began to think, what could I do to help the "layman"?

Simply following the trend, using stops and keeping risk within reason would not only help to mitigate large losses, but would put the layman on a course for profitability.

Two years have passed, and I still see people making the same mistakes. What I offer you here is an alternative that I believe provides a blueprint for success. It is a simple approach, but before we jump in you are going to have to change the way you think about Wall Street and possibly unlearn a few things. You will also need to learn a little about yourself.

Contents

Acknowledgements

As I said in my prior books, in markets, many come to the same conclusion through observation and experience. Often, I'll come up with what I think is a unique discovery only later to find out that others have come to the same conclusion many years prior. I have striven to give credit to all that have influenced me. For those who have come to similar conclusions and are not recognized, I can assure you, it's simply an oversight and I apologize.

What started out a small, very basic book on trading grew into a comprehensive guide over a course of 2 years. The unforeseen magnitude of the project necessitated involving more and more people. So many people were involved that I'm sure I'll overlook someone. Again, I can assure you, it's simply an oversight and I apologize.

To my parents for everything.

To Mike Adams for being a lifelong friend.

To my clients and those who read my articles and watch my webcasts. You inspire me to become a better trader.

To Larry Connors for giving me confidence in my research in my early years when I had none.

To Jeff Cooper for teaching me how to read charts.

To fellow traders who have helped and inspired me over the years including but certainly not limited to Joe Corona, Linda Raschke, Derrik Hobbs, Charles Kirk and Greg Morris.

To Dave Mecklenburg for helping me directly with content, editing, and especially for all his work "behind the scenes."

Early in the process, I asked for "guinea pigs" to allow me to test my vision for this book. These people graciously waded through rough drafts of often incoherent thoughts and provided me with feedback. They include Ken Stiltner, Gary Marsh, and John Crowe. I'd especially like thank fellow trader Michael Hart who not only provided opinions on content but also provided free editing on early drafts. Along those lines, I'd also like to thank Max Knobel for lending her opinion as a trader and technical writer. And to, my British friend Adam Rodgers. It was nice having someone who speaks "English" review the early text.

To my daughters, Suzie and Isabelle, for showing me what's really important in life.

To Randy Schneider for providing graciously providing free feedback and editing of the galley version.

To Julie Peterson-Manz for spending hours and hours with me working on the text, especially with the early chapters and trader's psychology. She's just a few hours short of being a co-author.

To Adrian Manz for agreeing to publish this book and for putting up with me in the process.

To Sean Katz of Scatter Design in Agoura Hills, CA for providing an outstanding layout and cover design.

To Worden Brothers for permission to use Telechart Platinum charts in this book.

And last, but certainly not least, to the Layman who inspired me to write this book.

SECTION I
First Steps

CHAPTER 1

Changing the Way You Think About Wall Street

You need to change the way you think about Wall Street. You can make better decisions than billionaires, insiders, television gurus, and "the pros." In the next few pages, I bust some Wall Street myths and highlight some truths. I will show why you should forget about conventional wisdom and will shake up what you think you know about trading the markets. Making this change is not difficult if you are willing to also change the way you think about yourself.

WALL STREET MYTH 1:
THE MARKET ALWAYS GOES UP LONGER TERM

It seems to be universally preached that the market "always goes up longer term." And, all you have to do is buy a diversified mutual fund or index fund and wait. The problem is that markets do not always go up longer term. Well, I suppose it all depends on what you mean by longer term.

Suppose you bought stocks in 1929 at the market peak. Provided you could have held through a 90% loss, it would then have taken you a quarter of a century just to get back to breakeven (Figure 1.1)

Figure 1.1 ~ Dow Industrials   *Chart Created With Telechart Platinum*

Let's say you bought stocks in the mid-1960's. Your return would have been almost zero until the market finally broke out in 1983, which was 17 years later (Figure 1.2)

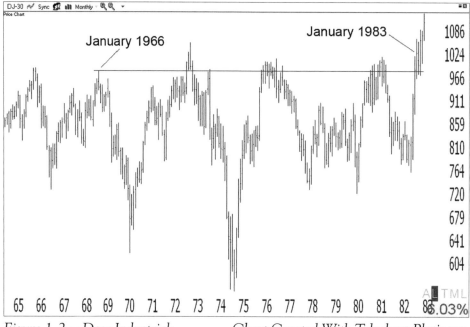

Figure 1.2 ~ Dow Industrials   Chart Created With Telechart Platinum

When I began this chapter, I was concerned that there might be a "that was then, this is now" mentality. After all, the benchmark S&P 500 wasn't far below breakeven from the 2000 peak. I thought I was going to have to make a strong case for not buying and holding. Unfortunately for the buy and hold crowd, the market made my case for me. The bear market that began in late 2007 would turn out to be the worst since 1929. By March 2009, the S&P was at 13-year lows. From these lows, the market will have to rally over 200 percent just to get to breakeven.

At more than one cocktail party, I have had people laugh in my face when I tell them that the market can go 25 years or more without going up. This has made for some heated discussions and awkward social situations. I have since learned from Dale Carnegie and my wife Marcy to just nod my head and enjoy my drink. Do not take my word for it, just look at the charts and grab me a Black and Tan while you are at it!

WALL STREET MYTH 2:
EXPERTS KNOW EXACTLY WHERE THE MARKET IS HEADED

It amazes me that "market gurus" will talk with total certainty. People often tell me that they bought a stock because someone on television was convinced that the stock had bottomed.

Consider this: In order to know with absolute certainty that a stock has bottomed, you'd have to know everything in the world. You'd have to know that the CEO is not going to drop dead of a heart attack and, if you did know, you'd have to know that an even better one would come along. You'd have to know that he's not going to get involved with a prostitution scandal, fudge the books, or embezzle from the company. Trust me, "it" happens. You'd have to know that a hedge fund with a large holding in the company will not only continue to hold the stock, but will buy even more. You'd have to know that all of those with much smaller positions — from those holding odd lots to little old ladies with mutual funds that have the stock in their portfolio — are not going to sell. You'd have to know that there will not be any more terrorist attacks. You'd have to know that the economy will remain strong. You'd have to know that there will be no government intervention or change in laws that are currently favorable to the company. The list goes on and on. The bottom line is, in order to predict with absolute certainty you'd have to know EVERYTHING.

WALL STREET MYTH 3: GOOD FUNDAMENTALS MAKE FOR GOOD INVESTMENTS

Has this ever happened to you? You own a stock. The company announces great earnings. You are excited. You watch in horror as the stock drops sharply. So what happened? Evidently, Wall Street has discounted those earnings and was hoping for even better earnings. Actual fundamentals do not matter for trading. Of course, a company will eventually have to make a profit. Otherwise they will run out of money and have to close the doors. However, "eventually" can be a long time. Stocks can trend higher for months or even years as long as the hope for good fundamentals stays alive. In fact, you will find that some of the best performing stocks have the absolute worst fundamentals — at least for the periods where their performance was the best. Conversely, stocks with great fundamentals can trend lower for extended periods of time. At some point they might be perceived as a value and begin to trend higher, but there is no guarantee. In the meantime, the economy could worsen, their products could become obsolete, competitors can arise, or a bear market could come along. Again, fundamentals do not matter for trading. The perception of them does.

Back to our layman's position in Apple Computer, on January 22, 2008, Apple reported that CEO Steve Jobs said, "we're thrilled to report our best quarter ever, with the highest revenue and earnings in Apple's history." The stock imploded over the next few weeks (Figure 1.3).

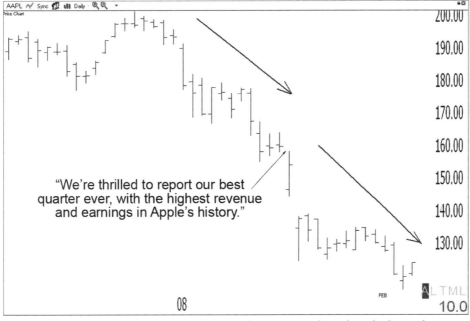

Figure 1.3 ~ AAPL   *Chart Created With Telechart Platinum*

WALL STREET MYTH 4:
BUY LOW AND SELL HIGH

We all know the old Wall Street adage "buy low and sell high." The problem is, no one knows what "low" is and if a stock is trading at low levels chances are that it has been trending lower and will continue to trend lower.

Thousands of stocks that seemed "low" in 2008 were substantially lower in 2009. Here is one example: On April 28, 2008, billionaire tycoon Kirk Kerkorian through his investment company Tracinda offered $8.50 for 20 million shares of Ford Motor Company. This must have seemed "low" to Mr. Kerkorian. After all, this was well off the all-time high of almost $39 per share.

An $8.50 share price represented nearly an 80 percent discount in Ford's stock, yet just a few months later, the company's shares were trading at just over $2 per share, bringing Mr. Kerkorian's losses to nearly $125 million. What's worse is that on October 21, 2008, Tracinda announced that they would be selling their stock. This action helped to further erode share price (figure 1.4).

Attempting to buy low is a loser's strategy. As you will soon see, you are much better off buying high and selling higher.

Figure 1.4 ~ F   *Chart Created With Telechart Platinum*

WALL STREET MYTH 5:
BUY STOCKS THAT HAVE A GOOD DIVIDEND YIELD

On July 17, 2008, I received a phone call from a neighbor. "Hey Dave, it is Bill, I am over at Ted's helping him work on his cow fence. Anyway, he wants to know what you think about GKK." I pulled up the chart (Figure 1.5) and saw that it had headed lower for a long time and had lost 75 percent of its value over the last year. Further, I saw that the trend had persisted lower in more recent times. So I told Bill to tell Ted that it was in a downtrend and should be avoided. I overheard Ted in the background making his case.

Figure 1.5 ~ GKK   *Chart Created With Telechart Platinum*

For some reason, when my friends ask for an opinion, they are not seeking the truth. They've already made up their mind or worse, like the layman, they have already taken a huge position. Therefore, I realized that anything else I would say would be ignored, so I decided to get more blunt. "Bill, tell him it is a piece of crap" (something they could smell from where they were standing). Ted then took the phone and began pleading his case. He cited the dividend yield of 12 percent. I explained to him that there is a reason the yield is so high. The chart does not lie. The stock is in a sharp downtrend and obviously in trouble. Something's wrong. They probably will not be able to keep paying that dividend and even if they could, it is likely to continue trending lower. "What you make on the dividend will likely be more than offset by the loss in the stock." He then continued to try to persuade me that the stock was a good buy, citing other fundamentals.

The stock continued to implode, losing over 95 percent of its value over the next few months. Even if the stock could continue paying the dividend, it would take over 15 years of dividends just to get to breakeven from these levels.

WALL STREET MYTH 6:
YOU CAN'T GO BROKE TAKING A PROFIT

"You can't go broke by taking a profit." Bull! This is how many people do go broke. They take many small gains and then one or two big losses wipes out all of those gains. There is an old commodity adage that says "Do not eat like a bird and defecate like an elephant." Simply put, this means do not take a lot of small gains and then wipe them out with a big loss.

Make sure you have a money management and position management plan that keeps risk in line but also allows for the potential for longer-term gains. More on this later, for now, just accept the fact that you can go broke taking a profit.

WALL STREET MYTH 7:
THERE IS A REASON THE MARKET IS GOING UP OR DOWN

It amazes me that the media will tell you daily exactly why the market went up or down. They infer that there is always a direct reason as to why stocks rise and fall. By this logic, all you have to do is learn the correlations. The problem is, often there aren't any. On Monday, the market dropped "because oil prices rose." On Tuesday, oil prices reverse, but stocks ignore this and continue to slide. The media quickly comes up with a new reason. On Wednesday, oil prices soar, but stocks ignore this and have a big rally. The media finds another reason to explain this, once again ignoring the fact that stocks rose in spite of rising oil prices. On Thursday, oil trades only marginally higher and stocks implode. The media then returns back to the rising oil reasoning.

More often than not, there is no reason why stocks rise or fall. They trade on emotions, period. Don't confuse the issue with the facts.

WALL STREET MYTH 8:
IT IS ONLY A PAPER LOSS

There is no such thing as a paper loss. A loss is a loss. Many think that a loss is only a loss if you "take it" by exiting the stock. I can assure you that a loss is a loss. If you are losing big on a stock, then you must exit. Yes, there is a chance that it will come back. But there is also a chance that it will not. What's worse is that if a stock is dropping, then chances are that it could be a trend. Therefore, there is a good chance that it will worsen.

Your account balance is your account balance, regardless of whether you have positions on or not. You can't show a creditor your account and explain to them that it is really worth another $100,000 because these stocks will come back and that these are only "paper losses." A loss is a loss. Unless you are Bill Clinton, what is, is.

WALL STREET MYTH 9:
TECHNICAL ANALYSIS IS MUMBO JUMBO

In its most basic form, technical analysis is simply the use of charts to help predict the market. Charts are used in every business. I am not sure why so many refuse to use them in stocks.

There is nothing magical about each little daily bar. It simply reflects how the stock traded that day based on the buying and selling of the market's participants. If a large institution makes a trade it becomes part of the chart. If a well informed insider makes a trade, it becomes part of the chart. Therefore, a chart reflects the trading of all market participants, from the large institution to the layman. You may not know what these participants are going to do next, but you can plainly see exactly what they have done. The patterns reflect the psychology of what they, and others, are likely to do next.

WALL STREET MYTH 10:
THE MARKET IS ALWAYS OKAY

Bad news might sell newspapers, but it will not get you a job as a television stock commentator. You do not want to turn on the financial news to hear that stocks are headed lower. You want to hear someone say that the worst is over and that you should hold on to your stocks because "they will come back." I have personally witnessed this upside bias. On more than one occasion, I have had my own bearish article headlines changed by editors to read less negatively. Sometimes, they have even been made bullish. It is okay to watch the financial news. Just remember that there is an upside bias even, and often especially, when the market is obviously doing poorly.

WALL STREET MYTH 11:
THERE IS ALWAYS A BULL MARKET SOMEWHERE

"There is always a bull market somewhere" implies that if you look hard enough, you can find stocks to buy regardless of market conditions. 2008 busted this myth. From the beginning of the year to the low hit on November 20, 2008, the S&P 500 lost nearly 50 percent of its value. During this same period, all sectors, as tracked by the Morningstar Industry Groups, were down. The majority of these sectors (64 percent) were actually down much more than the market itself. Further, those that were down the least had suffered much worse losses earlier in the year. It is true that occasionally selected areas, usually commodity related stocks, can trade counter to the market. However, there is not "always a bull market somewhere."

WALL STREET MYTH 12:
SHORTS ARE THE ROOT OF ALL EVIL

Markets go up and markets go down. If you are going to survive the markets longer term, you must be willing to play both sides.

Someone once said that anything good is illegal, fattening, or morally wrong. When markets are headed lower, shorting is good. It is not illegal or morally wrong and certainly not fattening — although it can fatten your wallet if done properly. Short sellers often get the blame when markets are headed lower but rarely do they get credit when their buying, also called covering, provides liquidity to help to dampen market meltdowns. In fact, in 2008 when the SEC tried to restrict shorting activities, it actually had a reverse effect. It exacerbated the slide (Figure 1.6). With fewer shorts in the market, there was no one left to buy. The market then fell on its own weight.

Figure 1.6 ~ S&P 500   *Chart Created With Telechart Platinum*

Many people have a problem with selling before buying. It just seems to fly in the face of what is natural. After all, how can you sell something that is not yours? The reality is that short-selling occurs in the real world all the time. Suppose a salesman sells you something that he does not have on hand. He is now "short" the product. As long as he can deliver your order for less than what you have agreed to pay for it, he makes a profit.

Short selling stocks is a similar process. If you believe a stock is headed lower, you put up a deposit to cover potential losses and instruct your broker to sell the shares short. To do this, he borrows the shares from another account and sells them in the market. You are now short the stock. As long as you can buy it back at a lower price, you will make a profit. Do not worry about mechanics of all this. Once your account is approved for shorting, you simply place your orders and click the "sell short" button instead of the "buy" button. If the stock is not available to borrow, you will receive a notice from your broker and the order will be canceled.

WALL STREET TRUTH 1:
STOCKS SLIDE FASTER THAN THEY GLIDE

There are a few Wall Street adages that are true. They do slide faster than they glide. It takes a lot longer to build something than to destroy it. Stocks are no exception. Therefore, you must be willing to exit at a modest loss because modest losses can quickly become huge losses.

The good news is that you can use this tendency to your advantage by shorting stocks, especially in bear markets. If you are willing to short stocks you will not only survive the next bear market, you will likely profit from it.

WALL STREET TRUTH 2:
MARKETS TRADE ON EMOTIONS

Stocks trade on emotions, period. They do not trade on reality. Stocks trade on the perception of reality, which is driven by human emotions. From the large institution down to the layman, the buying and selling of stocks is based on fear and greed — that is emotion.

So how do you read these emotions? You simply look at the charts.

WALL STREET TRUTH 3:
AVOID TRADING ON TIPS

Since I am "in the business," people feel compelled to give me tips. On many occasions, I have been pulled aside at social events, where someone speaks in a "hushed tone" that's somehow loud enough for those standing nearby (and not so nearby!) to also hear. From personal experience, 99 percent of the "tips" turn out to be false. And, of those that are true, they never turn out to be as great as claimed. For instance, I once received a tip that a stock would be taken over. And sure enough, the following trading day, it was. However, the price paid was several dollars lower than the previous day's price. This is what is known as a "take under."

Here's my favorite example from 2008. I received a tip from an oilman that Cheniere Energy (LNG) was to be taken over. And, if for some reason they weren't, they had huge undisclosed reserves that would make the company worth many times the share value. The stock then proceeded to lose over 90 percent of its value (see figure 1.7).

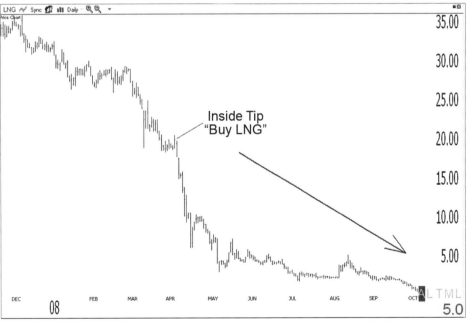

Figure 1.7 ~ LNG   *Chart Created With Telechart Platinum*

The bottom line is avoid tips. More often than not, they are wrong. Even if they are right, the payoff often is not as great as advertised. Further, if it truly is inside information, then it is illegal. Do not take my word for it, ask Martha.

WALL STREET TRUTH 4:
NEVER AVERAGE DOWN

In theory, all you have to do is double your bet every time a stock drops. Then, as soon as it comes back, you will make back all your money and then some. This is, provided that, the company does not go out of business and the stock comes back and you do not run out of money in the process. Those are three big "ifs." In 2008 many well known public companies filed for bankruptcy including a brokerage established in 1850 and a bank founded in 1889.

Those who are successful in life and business didn't get that way by "throwing good money after bad." However in the markets, some of these same people do just that.

WALL STREET TRUTH 5:
THERE IS NO HOLY GRAIL.

In spite of all the hype from system sellers, there is no holy grail. All systems are prone to losses. No system is immune.

By now, you are probably thinking, "Wait - aren't you selling us a system in this book?" No, I am offering a common sense approach to the markets. I am not guaranteeing that there will not be losses. In fact, occasional losses are one thing that I can guarantee. What I am proposing is that by following the trend and keeping risk in line, you can mitigate these losses and position yourself for longer-term success.

WALL STREET TRUTH 6:
IF YOU ARE SMART, IT IS GOING TO TAKE A LOT LONGER

"I haven't seen much correlation between good trading and intelligence.....
Many outstanding intelligent people are horrible traders. Average intelligence is enough."
- William Eckhardt

"You are nothing but a trend following moron"
- name withheld

If you are reading this book, you are of above average intelligence. How do I know this? First, fields with the potential for large gains attract the brightest of minds. The second reason is not as flattering. When it comes to the markets, the vast majority of the population does not read. They depend on the television media for their education. Unfortunately, the aforementioned unrelenting positive bias and constant "logical" correlations to news and fundamentals can make for very costly lessons. But I digress. My point is that since you've gone one step above watching TV for your trading education. I can say with a high degree of certainty that you are above average intelligence.

Before you start patting yourself on the back, I have some bad news. Since you are smart, it is going to take a long time to become successful in the markets. Unless you happened upon oil in your back yard, every success in your life has likely been approached with logic. In trading there often isn't any. You are dealing with the fear and greed of market participants. Markets trade on human emotions, not logic. Trying to figure out the reasons is an exercise in futility.

WALL STREET TRUTH 7:
YOU WILL HAVE TO DO YOUR HOMEWORK

With my approach to the market, you do not have to watch a screen all day. In fact, I recommend that you do not. You will have to do your homework though. This means studying the market indices, the sectors, and stocks.

If you want to become a better musician, you are going to have to practice your instrument. And, if you want to be a good chart reader, you will have to look at a lot of charts. Again, you will have to do your homework. Although homework has the word "work" in it, do not be alarmed. It is actually quite fun. For me, it is like being on a treasure hunt.

WALL STREET TRUTH 8:
EVEN EXPERTS AND "SMART MONEY" CAN BE WRONG

Earlier I showed that an "informed oilman" could be wrong. What if you were the most famous oilman of all time? Well, T. Boone Pickens lost over a billion dollars betting that the price of oil would rise in 2008 (Figure 1.8).

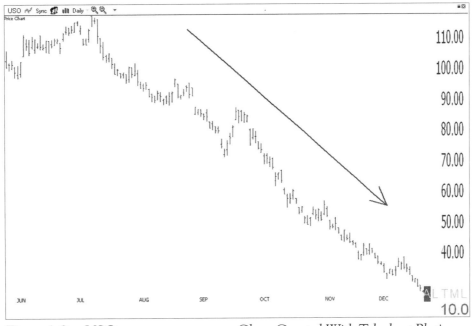

Figure 1.8 ~ USO   *Chart Created With Telechart Platinum*

So, if the most famous oil man of all time can't even make money in oil, how can the layman? It's simple. You have to learn to believe in what you see and not in what you believe. Drawing arrows on your charts will keep you from fighting trends. Letting the market make the decisions for you will keep you in the market when you are right and get you out when you are wrong. Most importantly, you will avoid the emotional pitfalls of forcing your own will onto the market.

So if it's that easy, why isn't everyone doing it?

That's a good question. It seems that people like a bargain. If a stock looks good at 50, then it is "on sale" for 40. And when it drops to 30, it is an even better deal. This bargain hunting causes people to fight trends. They not only refuse to give up even though the stock is obviously headed lower, they buy even more. This compounds their losses.

It is human nature to try to outsmart the market. Everyone to whom I have taught trend following during trending markets has been almost instantly successful. They tend to think that trading is easy. Greed begins to rear its head and they begin trying to outsmart the market to become even more successful. They start entering before trends begin. They try to pick tops and bottoms and exit long before the trend ends. When they hit the inevitable string of losses they assume that trend following no longer works. They start experimenting with other systems. Occasionally, they will get it right and hit a "sweet spot" where their new methodology matches the market. More often than not, this is short lived, and they began searching for yet another approach. They eventually end up perpetually "out of phase."

I never implied that trading was easy. However, I do believe with a little hard work and some common sense, you can be successful.

CHAPTER 2

Reading The Mind Of The Market Using Technical Analysis

When I began writing this book, I was concerned that it would be difficult for me to demonstrate why someone should trade stocks and not buy and hold them. I think 2008 made my case for me. The average mutual fund simply rode the market down. Sadly, this caused many to lose half of their retirement accounts. Conventional Wall Street wisdom is wrong. In order to survive the markets longer term, you must learn to think like a trader.

UNDERSTANDING THE BAR CHART

Thinking like a trader is not hard, provided you are willing not to try to outsmart the market. Markets trade on emotions. Fundamentals do not matter, at least for the period when a stock's performance is at its best. The only way to read the true emotions of the market is through technical analysis.

Technical analysis is a fancy way of saying "using price charts." In its purest form, the chart, and only the chart, is used. After years of searching, I consider myself a technical analysis purist. I've learned that you only need to focus on one thing — price. In fact, other than the occasional moving average, I do not use any indicators.

A price chart reflects the trading of all participants from the large institution down to the layman. You might not know exactly what market participants will do next, but you can see exactly what they have done. From this, you have a good idea of what is likely coming next. If you can understand the simple chart in Figure 2.1 you can learn to trade.

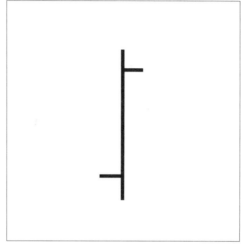

Figure 2.1 ~ Price Bar Chart

You don't have to worry about price-to-earnings ratios, dividends, cash flow, cash reserves, return on assets, or anything else on the company's books. You don't even have to worry about what the company does. The list of things that you don't have to worry about goes on and on. True, it is important to trade stocks whose sector is also trending, but that's it. If you can learn to understand Figure 2.1, you can become successful in the markets.

Let's look at what the price bar illustrates. For our discussion, all bars on the chart represent one trading day. The price bar in Figure 2.2 is a representation of four things: opening price, closing price, highest price, and lowest price.

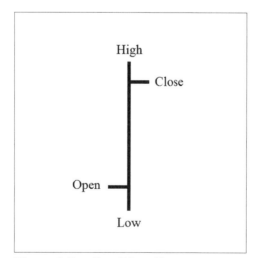

Figure 2.2 ~ Bar Chart Basics

The open is the price at which a stock begins the trading session. Although it can be, it is not necessarily the same price at which it closed on the prior day.

The close is the price at which a stock ends the trading session. If on Tuesday, the close is higher than it was on Monday, then there was more demand for the stock than supply. If the close on Tuesday is lower than Monday's close, then there was more supply for the stock than demand. As we'll soon see, where a stock closes within its daily range is also informative.

The high is the highest price recorded during the trading session. If sellers are reluctant to sell the stock then buyers will have to raise their bids. The more they are willing to pay, the higher the stock will go.

The low is the lowest price recorded during the trading session. If sellers are anxious to exit the stock and buyers are reluctant to buy, then the price will fall. The more anxious the sellers are, the lower the stock will trade. Sellers will have to reduce the price they are asking until they can find buyers.

The range (Figure 2.3) is the distance from the low to the high.

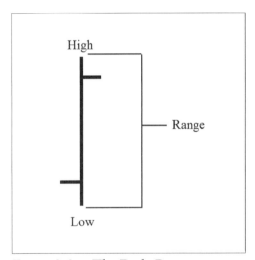

Figure 2.3 ~ The Daily Range

The narrower the range, the more traders agreed on price during the day. When this occurs, it forms what is illustrated in Figure 2.4 and is known as a Narrow Range Bar (NRB). Conversely, the wider the range, the less traders agreed on the price. When this occurs, it forms the bar shown in Figure 2.5 and is known as a Wide Range Bar (WRB). Keep in mind that some stocks are more volatile than others, so range is relative. A wide range bar in one stock won't necessarily be the same as what qualifies a wide range bar in a much more volatile stock. A stock's volatility is not a constant. Stocks heat up and they cool off. Wide range a year ago might only be considered a normal bar in recent trading.

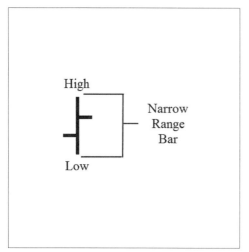

Figure 2.4 ~ Narrow Range Day

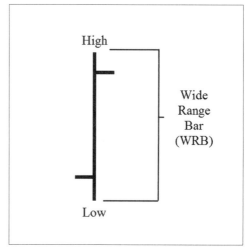

Figure 2.5 ~ Wide Range Day

A strong close (Figure 2.6) occurs when the last price is at or near the top of the range. This suggests there was demand during the day and more importantly demand late in the day. Late day buying indicates that traders were willing to carry the position overnight.

A weak close (Figure 2.7) refers to a close at or near the bottom of its range. This suggests excess supply during the day and, more importantly, late day supply. This indicates that traders were not willing to carry positions overnight.

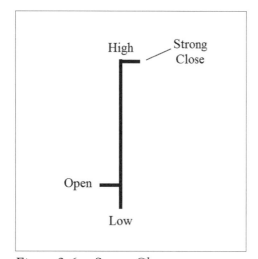

Figure 2.6 ~ Strong Close

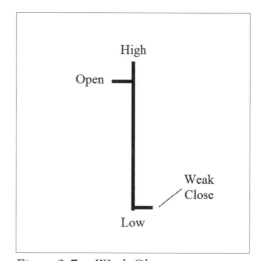

Figure 2.7 ~ Weak Close

Now, let's look at the relationship between the open and the prior close. Opens can be, but are not necessarily, the same as the previous close. News events can flow into the market overnight creating panic buying or selling. Opening price reflects these events as traders scramble to re-value a stock. Anxious traders are often quick to buy or sell regardless of price. Emotionally charged trading can create the exact high or low for the day. We can use this to our advantage.

A stock can do three things on the open: (1) open higher than the previous close, (2) open lower than the previous close, or (3) open at the same price as the previous close.

If the stock opens higher than the previous close but not higher than the previous high, it is known as a lap up. It opens within or overlaps the prior range. This is illustrated in Figure 2.8.

If a stock opens higher than the previous high, it is known as a gap up. This is illustrated in Figure 2.9.

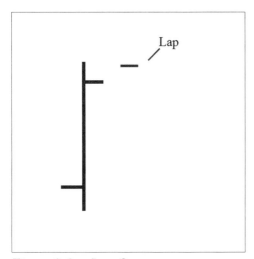

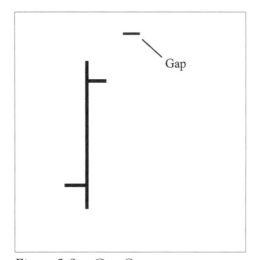

Figure 2.8 ~ Lap Open   *Figure 2.9 ~ Gap Open*

Lap ups and gap ups indicate that there was pent up demand coming into the trading day. Conversely, lap downs and gap downs indicate that there was pent up supply. Size matters. Large gaps and laps suggest an emotionally charged state. Traders want in or traders want out, regardless of the price.

Now, let's take a look at the relationship between where the stock opens and where the stock closes.

If the close is greater than the open (Figure 2.10), then there was demand during the day. This is especially true if the stock doesn't dip much below the open and then forms a wide-range up bar and closes strongly.

Conversely, if the close is less than the open (Figure 2.11), then there was supply during the day. This is especially true if the stock fails to trade much above the open and then forms a wide-range down bar and closes poorly.

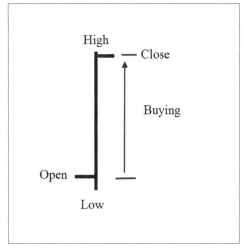

Figure 2.10 ~ Demand Day   *Figure 2.11 ~ Supply Day*

Now, suppose the opening and closing price are roughly the same (Figure 2.12). This suggests that by day's end, the buyers and sellers tended to agree on where the stock should be valued.

In summary (Figure 2.13), the open is where the stock begins the trading day and the close is where it ends. Buying (i.e. demand, bidding up the price) creates the high for the day and selling (i.e. supply, lowering the ask) creates the low.

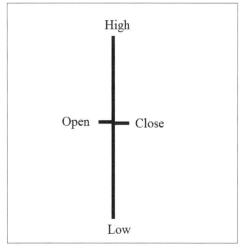

Figure 2.12 ~ Supply = Demand Day

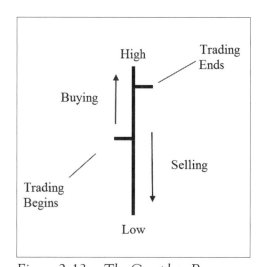

Figure 2.13 ~ The Complete Bar

EXAMPLE: A COMPANY MUSHROOMS

Portabella Mushrooms (BELLE) is a fictitious grower of Portabella mushrooms that has decided to capitalize on the popularity of the delectable fungus and go public. When a private company goes public, it is known as an initial public offering (IPO).

On the first day of trading, Monday, the stock opens at $10 and immediately moves higher. There is some initial excitement for the company. It never trades below the open, so the open and the low are the same. It hits a high of $10.50, but backs off a bit to close at $10.25. One bar doesn't give you enough information to make a trading decision, but it does tell you how the stock was initially received by the public (Figure 2.14).

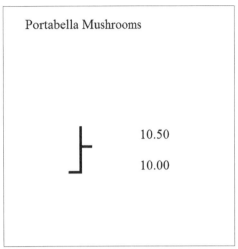

Figure 2.14 ~ Trading Day One

On Tuesday, the stock opens higher than the previous close, but not higher than the previous high, creating a lap. This tells us that there is some demand for the company. Traders decided overnight that they were willing to buy the company at a price higher than the previous close. Also notice that the open is once again the same as the low. The fact that the stock stayed at or above the open during the day suggests that this level was perceived as a value zone. Notice that the stock closed on its high. This action suggests that traders bought the stock all the way into the close, or at the least, there wasn't any late day selling (Figure 2.15).

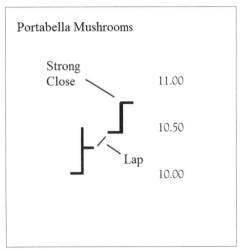

Figure 2.15 ~ Trading Day Two

On, Wednesday, the stock opens higher than the previous high, creating a gap higher. This suggests that traders are once again willing to pay up for the stock. The dip below the open is promptly met with buyers. The stock then rallied throughout the day, creating the widest range so far. It hits a high of 12 and only backed off slightly on the close. The fact that it didn't close on its high suggests that there was some selling late in the day. It did, however, managed to close near the high, suggesting that traders were once again willing to hold the stock overnight (Figure 2.16).

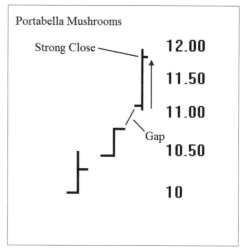

Figure 2.16 ~Trading Day Three

On the fourth day, Thursday, the stock gaps sharply higher. This action suggests that some traders wanted the stock regardless of the price. But this gap becomes the high of the day. This action suggests that those who previously owned the stock were willing to sell. The stock sold off hard to close at the low of the day. It also closed below the prior day's close. This action suggests that the stock might already be in trouble. Those who bought at the opening price are now in a losing trade. Those who bought near the highs of the prior day are now also faced with a loss. The weak close suggests that traders wanted out. They did not want to hold the stock overnight (Figure 2.17).

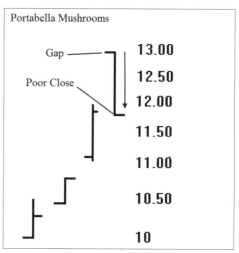

Figure 2.17 ~ Trading Day Four

The selling continues on Friday. Notice the stock gaps lower. This action suggests that traders want out regardless of price. The stock couldn't even rally above its open. It then sells off hard and closes poorly. This weak close suggests that traders did not hold the stock. Also, notice that BELLE finished only slightly above Monday's close. Nearly everyone who has bought it is now faced with a loss (Figure 2.18).

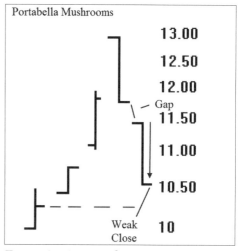

Figure 2.18 ~ Trading Day Five

The following Monday, the sixth day, the stock laps slightly higher and initially begins to trade higher. This action suggests that some bargain hunters are willing to buy BELLE. However, the stock soon finds its high and then sells off and closes poorly. It closes below where it initially began trading on the previous Monday. Now everyone, with the exception of those who bought the stock at the low of the day, is at a loss (Figure 2.19).

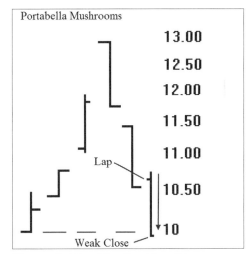

Figure 2.19 ~ Trading Day Six

The initial euphoria has worn off and BELLE begins to trade sideways (a). After all, it is only a food company. Although they taste great, how exciting can Portabella mushrooms be? The stock trades in a range between a low of $10 and a high of $10.50. The bottom of this range is perceived as a value zone or support. Near the top of the range, traders perceive BELLE as expensive and are willing to sell it. This is known as resistance (Figure 2.20)

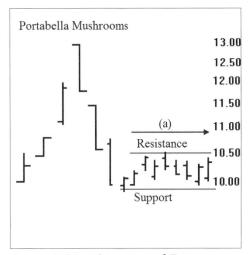

Figure 2.20 ~ Support and Resistance

We fast forward a week. We see that the stock continued to trade sideways (b), finding support near the bottom of its range ($10.00) and resistance near the top of its range ($10.50). When a stock trades sideways, bouncing between support and resistance, it is known as a trading range or a base. The longer the stock trades in a range, the more traders tended to agree upon price (Figure 2.21).

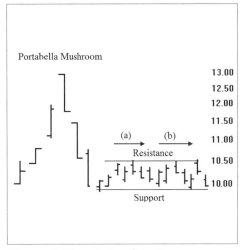

Figure 2.21 ~ A Trading Range

The stock begins to break down from its range. This prior trading range now becomes what's known as overhead resistance. Anyone who bought the stock during this trading range is now at a loss and will likely be looking to get out at breakeven. That is human nature. Therefore, it is important not to buy stocks when there is overhead resistance, also known as overhead supply. Otherwise, you might limit your gains (Figure 2.22).

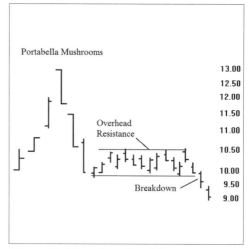

Figure 2.22 ~ Overhead Resistance

BELLE bounces off the $8.75 level then rallies back up to the overhead resistance. It has a hard time getting through this area. Likely, those who bought in that prior range are looking to get out at breakeven (Figure 2.23).

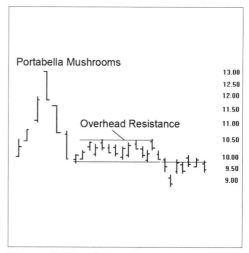

Figure 2.23 ~ More Resistance

BELLE sells off again, but again bounces off of the $8.75 level. Bottom pickers are looking to buy a bargain. Just because a stock is cheap does not preclude it from getting cheaper. The fact that it does bounce off the old lows suggests that this area could be support. When two lows are at or near the same level, especially when there is some trading in between, it forms what is known as a double bottom (Figure 2.24). I am not suggesting that you should trade this pattern. You are much better off waiting for a stock to show that it has the potential to rally from these classic technical patterns and then look for a place to enter. For now, just know that you should not attempt to pick tops or bottoms.

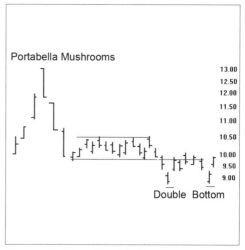

Figure 2.24 ~ Double Bottom

BELLE returns to its prior range and begins to trade back and forth within the channel. Then, the stock breaks out (Figure 2.25). Although it might appear that stocks should be bought when they break out of a range, keep in mind that more often than not, breakouts fail. True, there are some who trade breakouts successfully, but they have learned to live with the fact that there will be a high failure rate. As a trend trader, I like to wait to make sure that there is follow through and then look to enter after the first correction. This is provided that the stock shows signs of rallying out of that correction. In other words, I trade pullbacks.

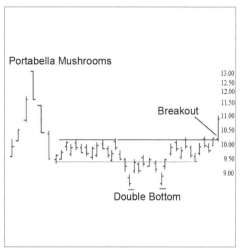

Figure 2.25 ~ Breakout

MUSHROOMS IN THE NEWS

I am now going to introduce some hypothetical news events for BELLE. I will demonstrate that technicals (i.e. the charts) can often lead the news. I am also doing this to show that the charts can also completely ignore or even trade counter to the news. Remember what happened to the layman with Apple?

There is often no direct correlation to the news and why a stock rises or falls. Stocks do not trade on reality. Stocks trade on the perception of reality. You only need the price to move in your favor to make a profit. Let me repeat: in order to profit from a trade, all that has to happen is that the price moves in your favor. It doesn't matter why. You do not have to worry about the news. Again, you only have to study price.

Price being driven by the perception of reality is what makes technical analysis great. Stocks often rise and fall long before the news "hits." Sure, the media will eventually try to explain why the stock moved, but many times a good trader will be long gone by then. Stocks can also move without news. In fact, some of your best trades will come from stocks with no news or even better, your stock trades counter to the news. People will always look for reasons. And in trading, there often are none. Attempting to apply logic to the market frequently puts investors on the wrong side of the price action. Again, all that has to happen is that the stock moves in your favor. It does not matter why! Don't confuse the issues with facts.

Now, getting back to BELLE, several days after its breakout, an article surfaces on how a fad diet which started in Asia is catching on in America. Supposedly, for every pound of Portabella mushrooms you eat, you will lose two pounds of fat.

BELLE rallies on, but stalls and reverses at its old highs. Those who bought at that high are now looking to get out at breakeven. This is known as a double top. The stock then sells off fairly hard. The trend ends as quickly as it began (Figure 2.26).

I am not suggesting that you trade these patterns directly. Rather, you can use them to build a case to buy or sell short the stock by combining them with the setups and concepts discussed later in the text.

A few days later, a report is released that shows that the fad diet doesn't work as well as advertised. Once again, the stock has led the news.

BELLE then finds support at the top of its prior base (a). It consolidates by trading sideways for a few days, and then once again begins to rally (b). This time, it manages to hit and close at all-time highs. Everyone who bought the stock and continues to hold it is now at a profit (Figure 2.27).

Soon after the stock makes new highs, a report is released that shows Portabella mushrooms can be processed into ethanol. With soaring energy prices, the stock begins trading more like an alternative energy company than a sleepy food company. The great thing about using technical analysis is that it will help you catch these paradigm shifts early.

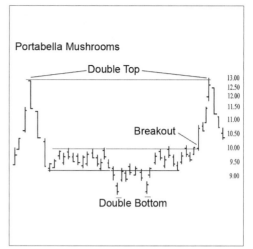

Figure 2.26 ~ The Double Top

Figure 2.27 ~ Support And New High

Notice the demand is so great that BELLE gaps higher, forms a Wide Range Bar (WRB) higher and has strong closes(Figure 2.28). These Trend Qualifiers give us clues about the nature of the trend. The stock pulls back (a). This can be due to profit taking from those who think that the trend has gone far enough. It can also be from eager shorts who can't believe that we'll all be running our cars on mushrooms soon. From the pullback (a), the stock begins to rally(b). Stocks often trend, pullback, and then trend again.

Energy prices continue to soar and so does BELLE. This, in spite of reports that the mushrooms aren't as great an ethanol source as once thought. Reports are being published that show that ethanol isn't all that it is cracked up to be anyway. The stock pulls back again (c), continues to ignore the news, and then accelerates higher (d) in spite of it.

The stock gaps sharply higher (e) as traders can't get enough. However, all good things come to an end. This turns out to be the exact high for the day and possibly for the stock itself. This opening gap quickly reverses forming what's known as an Opening Gap Reversal (OGRe).

The "Johnny-come-latelies" are now trapped on the wrong side of the market. The stock closes poorly and below the prior close. On subsequent days, the stock continues to implode and now has the same characteristics that it had on its way up, but in the opposite direction.

As a trend trader, you must be quick to recognize when trends are coming to an end. You can let the market make this decision for you through proper money and position management. If you are willing to accept the fact that markets go up and markets go down, you can begin looking for opportunities to profit should a downtrend emerge.

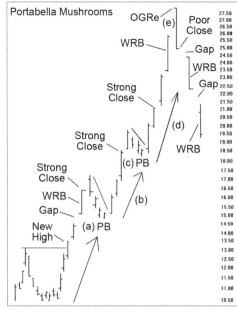

Figure 2.28 ~ Final Highs

THE RISE AND FALL OF EMPIRE RESOURCES

Now let's look at a real company, Empire Resources (ERS). Notice in Figure 2.28 that it exhibited many of the same chart and trending characteristics as our fictitious company, Portabella Mushrooms.

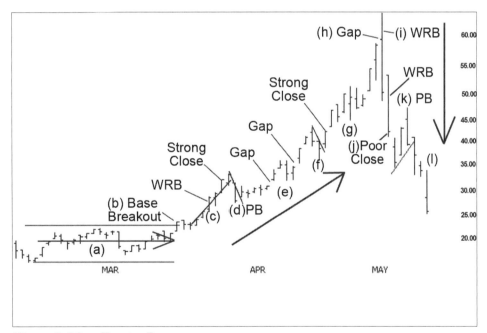

Figure 2.28 ~ Empire Resources

SUMMARY

Technical analysis in its purest form uses the price chart and only the price chart to predict price movement. All other factors are ignored. Price charts allow you to see exactly what market participants have done. There is no guarantee as to what they will do next, but based on their prior behavior, we have a good idea of what market participants will most likely do next.

CHAPTER 3
Trading For Both Short And Long-Term Gains

When predicting the weather, the longer your forecast, the tougher it will be to get it right. If it is cloudy and thundering, chances are it is going to rain soon. However, this obviously does not mean it will be raining this time next week or next month. Similarly, although market forecasts are based on probabilities, predicting short-term moves is much easier than predicting the longer term. Furthermore, the longer you are in a market, the better the chances are that you are going to get soaked. Short term trading keeps risks relatively small due to limited length of exposure.

By now you are probably thinking that I am building a case for short term trading. I suppose that to some degree, I am. But even though short-term trading has advantages, it also has disadvantages. The biggest is that gains are limited by the brief exposure to the market. Big trends often take time to develop. The real money is in longer-term moves.

If long term trading has bigger opportunities but risks too much and short term trading has smaller risks but does not make enough, what is a trader to do? Simple, it is not a mutually exclusive decision. Why not trade for short-term gains but be willing to stay with a portion of the position as long as the market moves in your favor? This allows you to have your cake and eat it too.

Considering the above, I seek out stocks that have the potential for both a shorter and longer term gain. My goal is to capture a small, quick profit but keep a portion of the position as long as the market continues to move in my favor. Although I have been slotted as a swing trader, I like to see myself as a longer term trader with better timing and money management. Like Hanna Montana, my approach has the best of both worlds.

WHAT IS TRADING?

Before we get into a trading a methodology, let's look at what trading really is. Trading is simply buying a market at one level (a) and selling it at another (b). Your profit from the trade is simply (b) – (a) (Figure 3.1).

Figure 3.1 ~ A Long Trade

Trading can also be shorting a market at one level (a) and buying to cover at another (b). Your profit, is simply (a) – (b) (Figure 3.2).

Figure 3.2 ~ A Short Trade

Easy, huh? Well, obviously it is a little more complicated. However, when you boil it down, as long as you sell higher than you've bought or cover lower than you've shorted, you've made a profit.

If you ever find yourself getting bogged down in indicators or trying to outsmart the market, come back to the simple concept of what trading really is. Look for obvious trends and trade them. If there are none, don't do anything.

THE ART OF GOING SHORT

I want to emphasize the importance of playing both sides of the market. You will notice that in all of my setups, I have included at least one example on the short side. Markets go up and down. If you are going to survive the markets in the long run, you have to be willing to play both sides. As traders, we can use the fact that "they slide faster than they glide" to our advantage.

I try to avoid biases. I view a short trade no differently than I view a long. This does not mean that shorting is as easy as trading the buy side. You have to be more nimble. On the short side, markets often do not give you much time to enter. Once a position has been opened the short covering rallies can be vicious, often forcing traders to close out and then watch the trend resume without them. Further, although they occur automatically and behind the scenes, there are also some mechanics to deal with. Stocks must be borrowed before they can be shorted. If the stock cannot be borrowed, then it cannot be shorted. Your ability to short will depend, in large part, on the inventory your broker has access to. More on brokers in Chapter 7.

Critics of shorting point to the fact that your risks are unlimited. A stock purchased can only go to zero, creating a 100% loss. A stock sold short could theoretically rally forever, creating virtually unlimited losses. So, yes, in theory, your losses are unlimited but this will be your reality only if you are ignorant, obstinate and refuse to implement a money management plan by exiting if you are obviously wrong. Further, you would have to continue to add money to the account to cover the losses, because if you didn't, the broker would politely exit the position for you. This is known as a margin call.

TRADING TRENDS

"There is nothing new under the sun"
~ Ecclesiastes 1:10

Around the time my first book *Dave Landry On Swing Trading* was published, one of my critics called me a "Trend Following Moron." When I published my second book, *Dave Landry's 10 Best Patterns and Strategies*, another critic said, "Terrible waste of your money. . . the book can be boiled down to 1) Trade with the trend. 2) Enter following a pullback after resumption of the trend."

Well, it is been nearly 10 years since my first book was published and I am still a trend following moron. In fact, I have T-shirts and buttons they say just that. Although I have tweaked things a bit over the years, the methodology remains essentially the same: Trade with the trend and enter on a pullback. As you will see in the next few pages, I borrowed heavily from patterns from my prior two books (which were more trading manuals geared toward slightly more experienced traders). The fact that the basic patterns have not changed is actually a good thing. This means that 10 years from now, these same basic patterns will likely continue to work as they have for the prior 10. However, the application of the patterns has changed somewhat to accommodate market conditions.

As we get into recognizing and trading trends with pullbacks and my specific patterns, keep in mind that these patterns and concepts work well in all markets. Therefore, although this book is geared toward stocks, what follows can be used in any market. This includes indices, Forex, commodities, bonds, and stocks. True, some markets do tend to trend better and this is why I favor stocks. However, patterns are patterns and markets are markets. Human psychology remains the same in all the financial venues.

RECOGNIZING TRENDS

Next to keeping risks in line, the next three figures are the most important ones in this book. I suggest that you spend the next several hours studying each one very carefully until they become ingrained. Then, take the test at the end of the chapter. If you pass, you are well on your way.

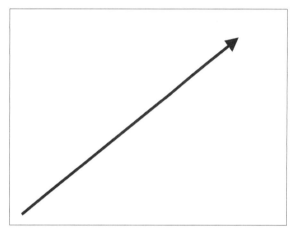

Figure 3.3 ~ Uptrend

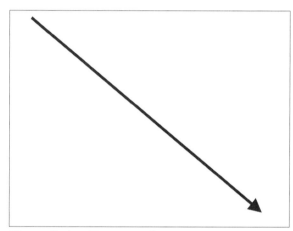

Figure 3.4 ~ Downtrend

Figure 3.5 ~ Sideways Market (No Trend)

THE TREND IS YOUR FRIEND

By now you are probably thinking, "Is this guy serious?" I can assure you that I am. You'd be surprised how many people who consider themselves trend followers are not. They fight obvious trends. The trend is your friend and it should be obvious. If, you find yourself in a drawdown, refer back to these arrows. Ask yourself, "Have I been fighting the trend? Or, have I been trying to see a trade when there is none?" You need to know your market. There are only three things the market can do: go up, go down, or go sideways. If the market is generally going up, then you should be buying stocks. If the market is generally going down, you should be selling stocks. And, if the market is going sideways you should stay flat, with no positions open.

So far we have established that trading is simply entering a market at one level (a) and exiting it another (b). I intentionally made both of the hypothetical charts in Figures 3.1 and 3.2 profitable trades to illustrate a point. Let's look at these two profitable trades one more time.

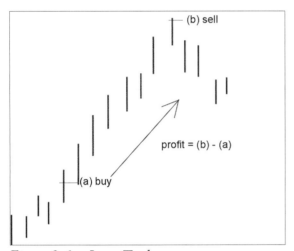

Figure 3.6 ~ Long Trade

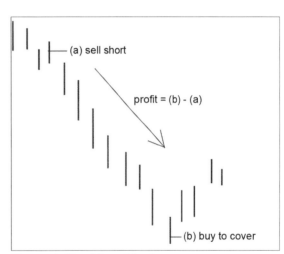

Figure 3.7 ~ Short Trade

Notice anything in Figures 3.6 and 3.7? I have added my famous arrows to the charts. The move from (a) to (b) in both charts is a trend. Therefore, even those who do not consider themselves trend traders actually are following the methodology for the time they are in the market. Let me repeat, they must follow the trend at least for the time that they are actually in the market. Otherwise, they would not have a profit. Since you must follow the trend for the time that you are in the market, my thinking is why not follow the trend all the time?

In addition to my favorite technique of drawing arrows to determine trend, there are other simple things that we can use to identify it.

First things first. Look at the chart to see if there is an obvious trend. Ask yourself, "Is the right side obviously higher than the left?" If the answer is yes, then the stock is in an uptrend. No? Then ask yourself, "Is the right side obviously lower than the left?" If yes, then the stock is in a downtrend. Once you have identified a trend look for further evidence to qualify it.

TREND QUALIFIERS

The great thing about markets that are trending is that they leave clues behind. I have dubbed these clues "Trend Qualifiers." They include persistency, base breakouts, gaps, laps, trend acceleration, wide-range bars, higher highs & higher lows, strong closes, new highs, and how much a stock moves over a given period of time on a percentage or point basis. The behavior of moving averages can also be used to help determine a trend. Let's break it down.

HIGHER HIGHS AND HIGHER LOWS

In its simplest form, an uptrend is series of higher highs and higher lows (Figure 3.8).

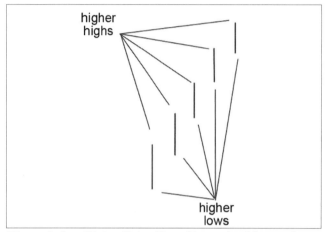

Figure 3.8 ~ Rising Price Bars Form An Uptrend

If you are not sure that whether or not a stock is trending, ask yourself, "Is it generally making higher highs and higher lows?" And of course, do not forget to draw your arrows.

THE POWER OF PERSISTENCY

Next to drawing arrows, my favorite way of qualifying trends is persistency. This refers to a market's ability to follow through from one day to the next. For those more mathematically inclined, this can be measured by complex statistical methods such as linear regression. The rest of us can simply look at the chart and draw a trendline through as many bars as possible (Figure 3.9)

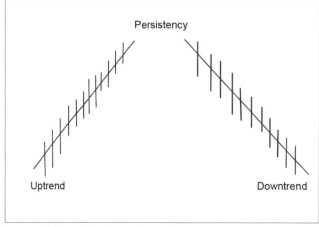

Figure 3.9 ~ Persistent Trends

INDIVIDUAL BAR PATTERNS

In Chapter 2, we learned that individual bars can often tell us about supply and demand A close higher than the previous close indicates that there is demand for a stock. Strong closes indicate that traders were willing to carry positions overnight. Gap ups and lap ups indicate there was pent up demand coming into the trading day. A wide-range bar, especially when the stock does not dip much below its open and closes strongly indicates that there was demand during the day. As these bars fit together, patterns and trends begin to emerge.

Let's look at the Trend Qualifiers in Empire Resources (ERS). Notice in Figure 3.10 that the stock traded mostly sideways (a) for several weeks. No trend here — hence the sideways arrow. Then ERS breaks out of its base (b). It soon begins to make higher highs and higher lows (c). This move persists for a week or so. During this time, the stock begins closing well and forms wide range bars higher, gaining over 10 points — nearly 50% from its breakout levels (b). ERS pulls back (d) and after a slow start, begins working its way higher again (e), generally making higher highs and higher lows. A brief pullback (f) and another push to highs (g). A gap higher (h) leads to sharply higher trade. Unfortunately, this turns out to be the exact top for the stock. It then sells off to close poorly, forming a wide-range bar lower (i). The following day it laps up but reverses to close poorly (j) on a wide-range bar down. Then, after a brief pullback (k), ERS resumes its slide (l). The stock goes on to make lower lows and lower highs.

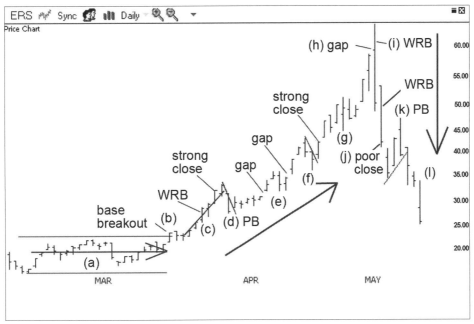

Figure 3.10 ~ ERS   *Created With Telechart Platinum*

MOVING AVERAGES

A moving average is simply an average of closing prices over a given period. A 10-day moving average is the sum of closes for the last 10 trading days divided by 10. The oldest data, in this case, 10 days ago, is dropped off when the next day is added in. The average "moves" with the price, hence the name moving average. Even the most basic charting programs have moving averages built in, so do not worry about the math.

Keep in mind that all indicators are a derivative of price. Therefore, with any indicator there will be some lag (i.e. delay). This is why I prefer looking directly at price. Lag aside, moving averages do have their uses. The concepts of Slope and Daylight (Figure 3.11) can be used to help alert you to a trend or to alert you to a gradual change in trend.

SLOPE

Slope is simply the angle of the moving average. An upward sloping moving average indicates an uptrend. A downward sloping moving average indicates a downtrend. And a flat moving average indicates that there is no trend.

DAYLIGHT

For uptrends, daylight occurs when the lows of the stock are greater than the moving average. This pulling away from the moving average suggests that the trend is in place and beginning to accelerate. This is especially true when combined with a positive slope.

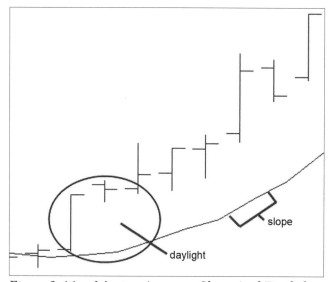

Figure 3.11 ~ Moving Average, Slope And Daylight

Now, let's take a look another look at ERS but this time, with a 10-day simple moving average. Notice in Figure 3.12 that the moving average was mostly flat while the stock remained in a sideways trading range (a). Then as the stock began to break out of the range it pulled away from the moving average, forming daylight (b) — the lows are greater than the moving average. Also notice as the stock climbed, the slope of the moving average became more and more positive (c). Notice that it stayed positive throughout the trend. Except for one "kiss" (d) of the moving average, there was daylight throughout the uptrend. As the trend ended and a new one began to emerge, the stock had daylight to the downside (e) (highs < moving average). Notice also that the moving average slope has turned negative (f).

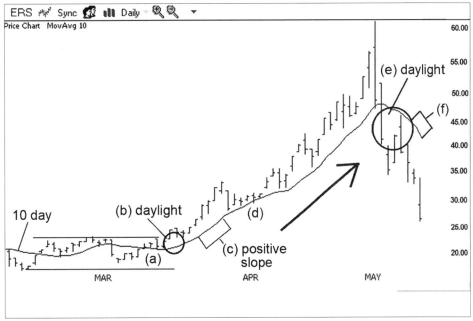

Figure 3.12 ~ ERS   *Chart Created With Telechart Platinum*

USING MULTIPLE MOVING AVERAGES

Proper order of multiple moving averages can also be useful when determining trend. For uptrends, this means that the shorter-term moving averages are greater than the longer-term moving averages. Notice in Figure 3.13 that I have plotted my three favorite moving averages: the 10-day Simple (10SMA), the 20-day Exponential (20EMA), and the 30-day Exponential (30EMA). I'll explain these further when discussing my Bowtie strategy. For now, just know that when shorter-term moving averages are above the longer-term moving averages (10SMA > 20EMA > 30EMA), it suggests an uptrend.

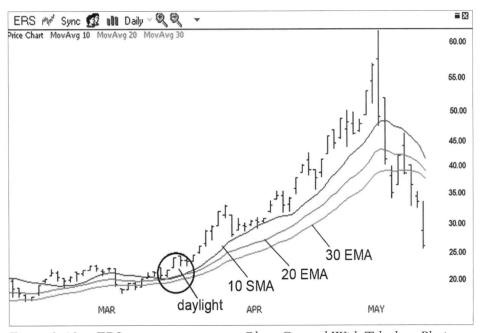

Figure 3.13 ~ ERS   *Chart Created With Telechart Platinum*

There is one caveat. As previously mentioned, all indicators have some lag. Therefore, during an abrupt change in trend, the moving averages will be slow to catch up. Notice in ERS that the moving averages are still in a proper uptrend (10SMA > 20EMA > 30 EMA) even through the stock has obviously rolled over. Keep this in mind when using moving averages. Study price action first and then add moving averages to help gauge the trend.

THE TREND SHOULD BE OBVIOUS

I am amazed at how many traders try to define a trend when there is none. The trend should be obvious. If the right side of the chart is higher than the left, then it is in an uptrend. If the right side of the chart is lower than the left, then it is in a downtrend. If you cannot draw a big arrow pointing in the direction of the trend, then it is probably not a trend. I realize that I have trivialized this with my "arrows" but the trend should be obvious!

THE MARKET: WHAT FLOATS YOUR BOAT?

"A rising tide lifts all boats" is one of the few Wall Street adages that is true. In a bull market, the majority of stocks go up. Conversely, in a bear market the majority of stocks go down. Therefore, trying to buy stocks in a bear market or sell short stocks in a bull market can be equated to swimming against the tide. Sure, it can be done, but the odds are stacked against you.

By now you should be aware that you should avoid listening to the media or analysts who would like to tell you which direction the market is headed. Your arrows are your best ally.

SECTORS: BIRDS OF A FEATHER

A sector is an index based on a group of similar stocks. Just as a rising tide lifts all boats, birds of a feather do flock together. If a sector is hot, the majority of the stocks within it will rise. If a sector is not hot, the majority within it will fall. It is important to make sure your sector confirms what you are seeing in the individual stock. This is especially pertinent since some sectors can occasionally trade contra to the overall market.

AN INTRODUCTION TO PULLBACKS

As stated earlier, one of my critics was able to boil my method down to two sentences illustrated in Figure 3.14.

1. Trade with the trend

2. Enter following a pullback after resumption of the trend.

By now, you should have a good understanding of what a trend is. If not, go back and study the arrows mentioned earlier in this chapter. A pullback is simply a correction of an established trend. This is healthy because it gives the stock some rest. It helps to shake out nervous longs and attracts some trend fighting eager shorts. If the trend resumes, the shorts are forced to buy to cover and the longs that were shaken out must buy again or risk being left behind. All this buying propels the stock even higher.

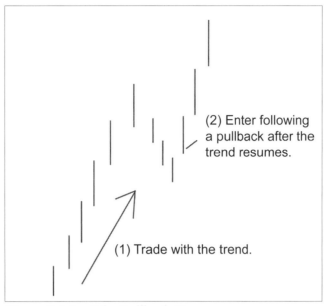

(2) Enter following a pullback after the trend resumes.

(1) Trade with the trend.

Figure 3.14 ~ The Pullback Entry

I am going to dissect pullbacks much further throughout the rest of this book. For now, if you understand my critic's two sentence explanation, then you understand my practical approach to the markets. The rest is just details.

IMPORTANT: Before we get into examples of pullbacks and my specific pullback patterns, keep in mind that what I am going to show you in the next few pages is the "textbook" way to trade them. For instance, to keep things simple, most examples are going to enter right above the high (for longs) or low (for shorts). In reality, unless conditions are really great, you would want to vary these entries a bit. Therefore, before attempting to actually trade pullback related patterns, I would encourage you to read through this entire book to make sure you understand important nuances. You should also paper trade the patterns for a while until you get a good feel for how they work.

EXAMPLES OF PULLBACKS

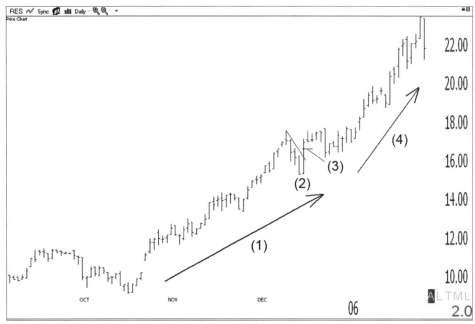

Figure 3.15 ~ RES   *Chart Created With Telechart Platinum*

1. In Figure 3.15, RPC Inc. (RES) is in a strong uptrend, gaining over 80 percent in less than two months. Notice other trend qualifiers such as a gap, a persistent and accelerating move higher, and of course, my favorite, a big up arrow.

2. The stock pulls back.

3. Enter as the stock begins to resume its uptrend.

4. The stock rallies over 50 percent over the next six weeks.

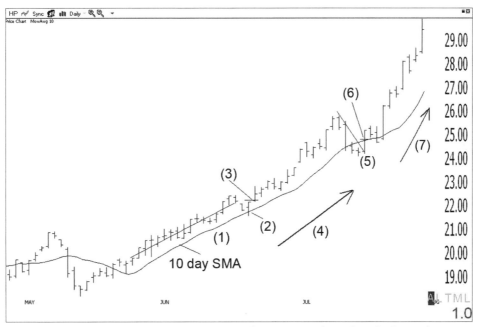

Figure 3.16 ~ HP   *Chart Created With Telechart Platinum*

1. In Figure 3.16, Helmerich & Payne (HP) begins trending higher. It is in a persistent trend, trading higher and higher day after day. It is trading above its 10 SMA. In other words, there is Daylight.

2. The stock pulls back and touches the 10 SMA. This is a Kiss MA Goodbye setup (discussed later). Because it is pulling back from a persistent trend, this is also a Persistent Pullback (also discussed later in this chapter).

3. Enter when the stock begins to resume its uptrend.

4. The stock resumes its uptrend, gaining over 15 percent over the next few weeks.

5. The stock pulls back to set up as another pullback. This is also a Kiss MA Goodbye setup.

6. Go long as the trend resumes.

7. The stock gains another 25 percent over the next two weeks or so.

Because of their limited trading history, IPO's can make great candidates for pullbacks. When a new issue is trending higher, there are no "bad memories." Everyone who already owns the stock is happy. Those who do not may be looking to jump on in order to not miss the boat.

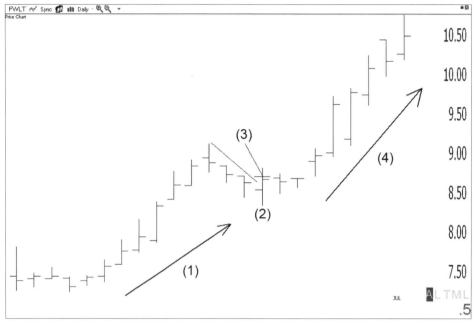

Figure 3.17~ FWLT   *Chart Created With Telechart Platinum*

1.   In Figure 3.17, Foster Wheeler (FWLT) is not met with much enthusiasm when it first goes public but it soon begins to trend higher.

2.   The stock has its first pullback.

3.   Go long when the stock begins to rally.

4.   The stock gains over 20 percent in less than two weeks.

Figure 3.18 ~ CIEN   *Chart Created With Telechart Platinum*

1.   In Figure 3.18, Ciena Corp. (CIEN) is in a downtrend. Notice that this is also a persistent downtrend.

2.   The stock pulls back.

3.   Enter as the trend resumes. Notice the entry I have shown is actually lower than a "textbook" entry which would have triggered two days prior. We will discuss advanced entry and exit strategies later in the text.

4.   The stock loses over half of its value over the next seven to eight weeks.

SPECIFIC PULLBACK PATTERNS

"One should not increase, beyond what is necessary,

the number of entities required to explain anything."

- Occam's Razor

"Simplicity is the ultimate sophistication"

-Leonardo Davinci

I spent many years searching for the perfect methodology. I would wake up early and stay up late knowing that if I worked hard enough, I would find it. I have tried every indicator that I could get my hands on. I went through numerous texts on technical analysis and spent many hours studying each and every indictor, oscillator, moving average convergence divergence, stochastics, Fourier Transforms, Relative Strength Index, and cycles. You name it, I tried it. Not only did I study these indicators carefully but I would even create new indicators from the indictors, making the complex even more complex. I have even studied arcane methods such as counting price bars and price waves. I was obsessed.

It took me many years to come to the realization that there is no holy grail — no method that will lead to eternal profits while avoiding all losses. More importantly, I learned that simple is better. Since the ultimate goal was to capture a price trend, I began to think I should focus on that. So I did. Little by little I began peeling away the indicators and focused more on price, seeking out trend. I reached a point where I was back to a blank chart. Again, other than the occasional moving average, I do not use any indicators.

Although not perfect, I discovered that the best way to enter a trend was after a correction, also known as a pullback. In addition to the aforementioned generic pullbacks, the following variations are the bread and butter of my methodology. They are used the majority of the time. For those interested in some of my ancillary and slightly more advanced patterns, see my prior books.

Start with one pattern and build. All you actually need is one pattern to be successful. I have many clients who prosper trading only one pattern. Master one setup and then start adding. Look at a lot of charts. Learn how to identify trend first and then look for these specific patterns. You will find with a little practice, the best setups will begin to jump out at you.

TREND KNOCKOUTS

Trend Knockouts (TKO's) are a simple yet effective pattern. They remain one of my favorites, especially when combined with persistency.

Those with very little money or patience will be quick to dump a market at the first sign of a correction. While it is a good idea to trade in the direction of the trend, I have learned you are much better off waiting until the weak hands are knocked out of the market before entering yourself. This reduces the probability of these traders dumping their positions and taking you out with them.

The knockout move also attracts, and can subsequently shake out, top and bottom pickers. TKOs work in both uptrends and downtrends. In uptrends, the knock out move attracts eager shorts who refuse to believe that the stock deserves its high valuation. They have confused the issue with facts. Should the trend resume, they will be forced to cover their short position. This buying helps to propel the trend even higher. In downtrends, the knock out move attracts eager bottom fishers who want to buy a stock while it is still cheap. Should the downtrend resume, these fickle traders will likely dump their position. This additional supply will exacerbate the slide.

Trend Knockouts (TKO's) identify strong trends from which the weak hands have already been knocked out. By placing your order above the market (or below for shorts), you have the potential to capture profits as the trend resumes.

Here are the rules for buys (Figure 3.19):

1. The stock should be in a strong uptrend and ideally, a persistent uptrend. Use trend qualifiers or moving averages to gauge trend. Do not forget to draw your arrows.

2. The stock should trade below at least the two prior lows. Ideally, this should also be on an expansion of range. In other words, it should be a sharp move lower — a wide range bar (WRB) down. This can occur just after the new high, creating a one-bar pullback or it can occur within several days of the new high, creating a TKO within a pullback.

3. Go long above the high of the knockout bar, and remember, no trigger, no trade.

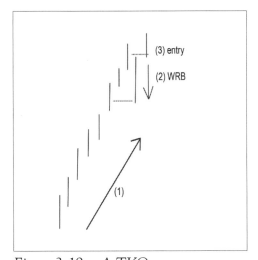

Figure 3.19 ~ A TKO

The bigger the move lower, the better the chance more players will be knocked out. There is one caveat. If the move is too extreme then one has to wonder if the trend may truly be coming to an end. In this case, the stock should be avoided. I realize that "too extreme" is somewhat arbitrary. However, with a little experience, you will know it when you see it.

The good news is, even if you do not, the chances of the stock triggering are very small after an extreme move lower.

One great thing about TKO's is that you can frequently trade them in a textbook fashion more than many other patterns. Your entry can often go right above the high and the protective stop can be placed right below the knockout bar.

Now, let's look at some examples of TKOs.

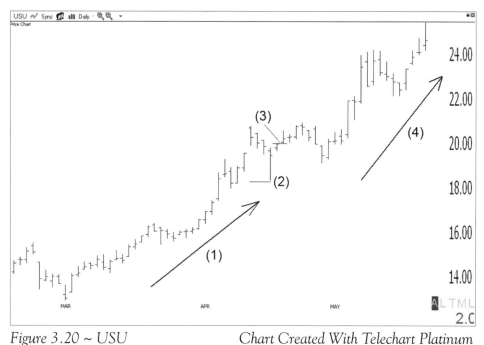

Figure 3.20 ~ USU   *Chart Created With Telechart Platinum*

1. In Figure 3.20, Usec (USU) is in a strong accelerating uptrend.

2. The stock begins to pull back and then has a sharp sell off, trading below at least the prior two lows. This is actually 4-day low.

3. Go long as the stock takes out the high of the knockout bar.

4. The stock resumes its uptrend.

Long before our layman's favorite stock began going down on good news, there were some very nice uptrends.

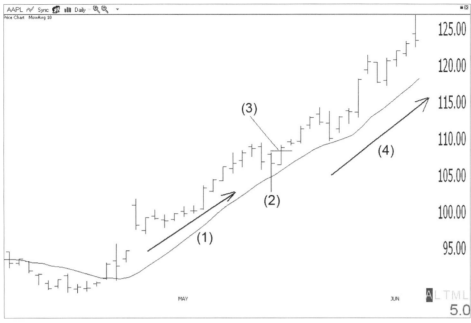

Figure 3.21 ~ AAPL   *Chart Created With Telechart Platinum*

1. In Figure 3.21, Apple (AAPL) is in an accelerating uptrend. Notice the Daylight and other Trend Qualifiers such as a gap, strong closes, and higher highs and higher lows.

2. The stock has a sharp sell-off. I have included the 10-day moving average to show that this is also a Kiss MA Goodbye setup (more on that later).

3. Go long as the high of the knockout bar is taken out.

4. The stock resumes its uptrend.

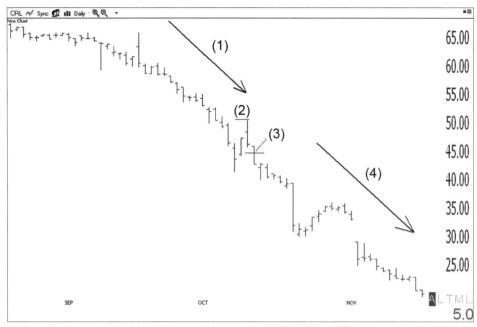

Figure 3.22 ~ CRL   *Chart Created With Telechart Platinum*

1. In Figure 3.22, Charles River Labs (CRL) is in a downtrend. Notice that this downtrend is persistent and accelerating.

2. The stock has a quick, sharp pullback. The second bar of the pullback takes out at least the prior two highs.

3. Go short as the stock takes out the low of the knockout bar.

4. The stock loses over half of its value over the next six weeks.

SUMMARY
In spite of their simplicity, TKO's can quite often be very profitable. Once a stock in strong trends has faked out weak players, it can often clear the way for you to profit.

PATTERN APPLICATION
Because they are a very common pattern, you have to be very selective. Only trade markets that are in obvious trends with obvious knockout moves. Persistent trends work best with the pattern. Further, the knockout move should be meaningful. Ask yourself, if I were long or short this market, would this TKO move have taken me out?

PERSISTENT PULLBACKS
I stated earlier that when analyzing trend, my favorite technique next to drawing arrows is to look for persistency. Persistency is simply a market's ability to follow through from one day to the next. This was illustrated in Figure 3.9. For those more mathematically inclined, this can be measured by complex methods such as linear regression. However, for the rest of us, we can simply look at the chart and draw a trendline through as many bars as possible.

An advantage of the Persistent Pullback is that it self regulates. This is especially true if you also require sector confirmation, which I highly recommend. In choppy markets, it is virtually impossible to find any stocks set up as persistent pullbacks. In bull markets, it is virtually impossible to find shorts. And in bear markets, it is virtually impossible to find longs. In fact, while working on this book, I studied thousands of charts from the slide that began in 2007 to the March lows of 2009. I could not find any buy side examples during this period.

This self regulating nature can be great for those new to trend trading. It keeps them on the right side of the market. And it keeps them out of the market during less than ideal conditions. This is why I suggest that those new to trend trading only trade persistent pullbacks until they gain confidence.

More experienced traders will find persistent pullbacks very useful when they find themselves fighting trends and overtrading during choppy markets. During these difficult times, I suggest that they return to trading only this pattern. This will put them back on the right side of the market and will keep them out during choppy conditions. In fact, on more than one occasion, I have suggested traders in a slump to do just that. Alternatively, when you find yourself having difficulties, you can pay me a lot of money to work one-on-one with you. Or, you could just exclusively trade Persistent Pullbacks until you regain your confidence.

Now, let's look at the rules for my Persistent Pullback pattern. This setup was originally published in my second book "*Dave Landry's 10 Best Swing Trading Patterns and Strategies*." Below are the rules for buys. Short sales are reversed. (Figure 3.23)

1. The stock should have moved one month, approximately 20 bars, in one direction. Ideally, a trend line drawn through the bars should intersect as many bars as possible. This can be done by hand or by using a linear regression trendline. During this period, the stock should have had made a significant move.

2. After Rule 1 has been satisfied, look to enter on a pullback or pullback related pattern. One of my favorite patterns that occurs out of a persistent move is a Trend Knockout (TKO).

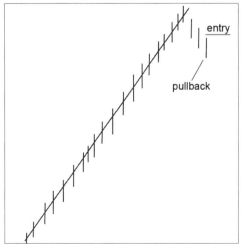

Figure 3.23 ~ Persistent Pullback

Let's look at some examples.

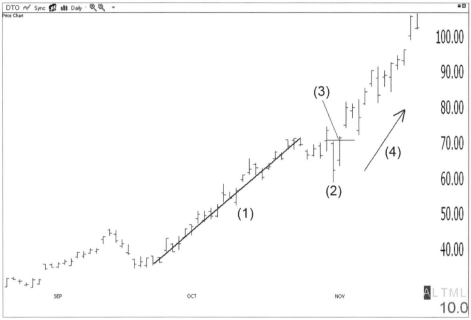

Figure 3.24 ~ DTO   *Chart Created With Telechart Platinum*

1. In Figure 3.24, the Double Short Crude Powershares (DTO) are in a persistent uptrend. Notice that a trendline drawn through the bars intersects virtually every one. During this period the stock rallies over 30 points, gaining over 80 percent.

2. The stock pulls back. The stock forms a Technical Knockout (TKO). For those familiar with my first book, *Dave Landry on Swing Trading*, you might also recognize this pattern as a Double Top Knockout (DTKO).

3. The stock triggers an entry.

4. The stock nearly doubles in value over the next month.

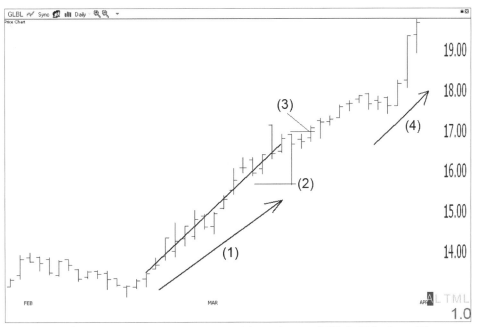

Figure 3.25 ~ GLBL   *Chart Created With Telechart Platinum*

1. In Figure 3.25 Global Industries (GLBL) is in a persistent uptrend, gaining over 30 percent in less than a month.

2. The stock has a sharp one day sell-off, forming a Trend Knockout.

3. Go long as the high of the knockout bar is taken out.

4. The trend resumes with over 18 percent in gains in two weeks.

Figure 3.26 ~ SHLD   *Chart Created With Telechart Platinum*

1. In Figure 3.26, Sears Holding (SHLD) is in a significant persistent downtrend. During this period it drops over 50 points, losing half of its value. A trendline drawn through the bars intersects virtually every bar.

2. The stock pulls back.

3. The stock triggers as entry.

4. The stock resumes its persistent downtrend, losing more than 50 percent of its value over the next three weeks.

SUMMARY

Persistent pullbacks are a very simple, very effective pattern. They are self regulating. You get more setups in good times and fewer setups in bad. This is especially true if you require the sector and the overall market to also be in a trend. Ideally these would also be characterized as a persistent trend.

Persistent pullback's self regulating nature helps keep traders on track. When discipline breaks down, persistent pullbacks force us to stick with the trends instead of fighting them. Most importantly, the pattern will keep us out of the market when it is trendless.

PATTERN APPLICATION

The pattern works equally well on the long and short side of the markets. However, because they "slide faster than they glide," you are more likely to find orderly persistent uptrends than downtrends. The best trades occur when the sector and overall market are also in persistent trends.

KISS MA GOODBYE

Many times I will come up with what I think is an unique discovery only to later find out that others have discovered the same thing, often many years prior. The Kiss MA Goodbye is one such pattern. In the mid 90's, I spent many hours studying the potential of trend following systems. Much of this research used only moving averages. One of these systems, the 2/20 EMA Breakout System, was published in the December 1996 issue of Technical Analysis of Stocks & Commodities. The system essentially looked for a breakout from the moving average. I began tweaking this, using daylight as a gauge for a trend followed by a pullback to the moving average. Around the same time, Larry Connors and Linda Raschke published *Street Smarts*. To my surprise, one of the patterns was very similar to what I had dubbed "Daylight Pullbacks." Therefore, to give credit where it is due, this pattern is very similar to Linda's "Holy Grail," with the main exception that I only use the concept of "daylight" to gauge trend whereas Linda uses an indicator.

To review, daylight simply means that the price has pulled away from the moving average. The lows are above the moving average for uptrends and the highs are less than the moving average for downtrends (refer to Figure 3.11). The pattern simply looks to define a stock that is in a trend using daylight and then looks to enter that trend when the stock pulls back to "Kiss the Moving Average (MA) Goodbye." Let's define this further using the concept of daylight with a 10-day simple moving average, available in virtually all charting packages.

Here are the rules (Figure 3.27).

1. The stock should pull away from its moving average for at least 10 days (fewer days are okay for strongly trending stocks). During this period, the lows must be above the moving average. In other words, there should be at least 10-days of daylight.

2. Wait for the stock to correct (pull back) to the moving average. The low must intersect the moving average.

3. Look to enter above the previous high (or highs).

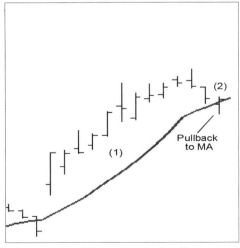

Figure 3.27 ~ Kiss MA Goodbye

Let's look at some examples.

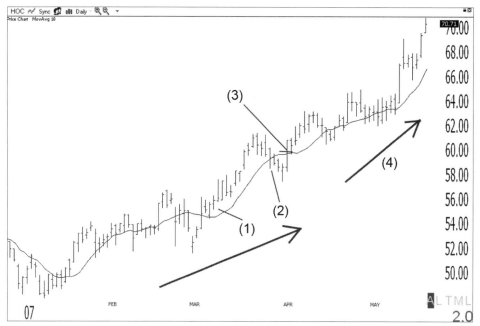

Figure 3.28 ~ HOC   *Chart Created With Telechart Platinum*

1. In Figure 3.28, Holly Corp. is in a longer-term uptrend. The stock begins to pull away from its 10-day moving average as the trend accelerates. Notice that it has at least 10 bars (13 total) of "daylight" where the lows are greater than the moving average.

2. The stock pulls back to its moving average.

3. Enter as the trend resumes.

4. The stock rallies over 20 percent over the next few weeks.

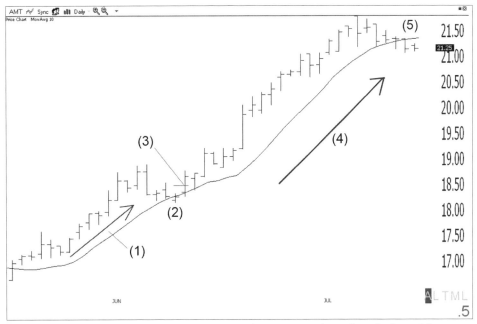

Figure 3.29 ~ AMT   *Chart Created With Telechart Platinum*

1. In Figure 3.29, American Tower Corp. (AMT) is trending based on the fact that at least 10 lows (16 total) are greater than the 10-day simple moving average.

2. The stock pulls back to its 10-day moving average.

3. Enter as the trend resumes. Those familiar with my prior work will also recognize this as Trend Pivot Pullback (originally published in *Dave Landry on Swing Trading, and Dave Landry's 10 Best Patterns & Strategies*).

4. The stock rallies over 16 percent.

5. The stock pulls back to give MA another kiss.

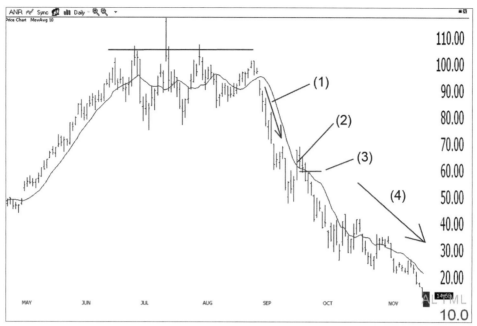

Figure 3.30 ~ ANR   *Chart Created With Telechart Platinum*

1. In Figure 3.30, Alpha Natural Resources (ANR) is in a downtrend as defined by 10 consecutive bars where the highs are less than the 10-period simple moving average. Notice that prior to this, the stock traded sideways after a longer-term trend, failing to make any forward progress. This clues you in to the fact that the prior uptrend may be ending.

2. The stock pulls back to the SMA. Notice in the pullback that the high intersects the moving average.

3. Enter as the trend resumes.

4. The stock resumes its downtrend, losing over half of its value over the next few weeks and nearly 70 percent of its value over the next few months.

SUMMARY

The Kiss MA Goodbye pattern is a defined pullback using only a simple moving average criterion. Once the trend is in place based on daylight, we look for a pullback to the moving average. It is a great pattern for newer traders since it takes the guesswork out of the trend and the correction. They are also easy to recognize visually.

PATTERN APPLICATION

I find that the pattern works equally well on both sides of the market. However, since "they slide faster than they glide", I prefer getting into shorts at the first possible chance. Therefore, I prefer transitional patterns (see Next Steps) for shorts. However, keep in mind that when the overall market is in an extended downtrend, virtually all stocks have also been trending lower. Therefore, there often are not any transitional trading setups left.

FINAL THOUGHTS FOR CHAPTER THREE

We've covered a lot in this chapter, but it can all be boiled down to a few simple concepts. In its purest form, trading is simply buying (or shorting) at one level and selling (or covering) at another. The trade is profitable if and only if you catch a trend. Since the ultimate goal is to catch a trend, seeking trends is the most logical approach to trading. Trends can be gauged with trend qualifiers and moving averages. They should be so obvious that you can draw a big arrow that points the way. Ideally, the overall market and stock's sector should confirm the trend. Once trends are identified, you should wait for a correction before looking to enter. In other words, we trade pullbacks. Specific pullback patterns such as Trend Knockouts, Persistent Pullbacks, and Kiss MA Goodbye are effective ways to recognize and trade pullbacks.

POP QUIZ (NO CHEATING!)

By now you should be able to recognize obvious trends. Take the following quiz and make sure. If you pass, then proceed. If not, re-read this chapter.

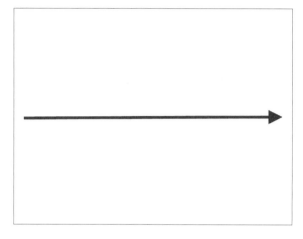

1. This is an example of:
   A. An Uptrend
   B. A Downtrend
   C. Sideways (No Trend)

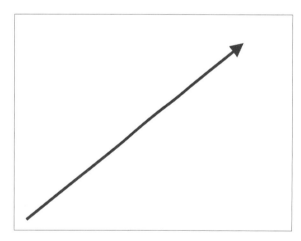

2. This is an example of:
   A. An Uptrend
   B. A Downtrend
   C. Sideways (No Trend)

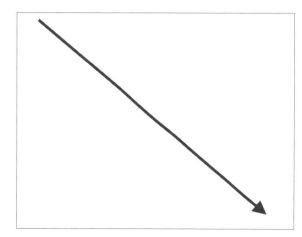

3. This is an example of:
   A. An Uptrend
   B. A Downtrend
   C. Sideways (No Trend)

Answer Key: 1 = C 2 = A 3 = B

CHAPTER 4

Trading Pullbacks: The Details

By now you should understand how to recognize a trend. After identifying the trend, you should be able to spot basic pullbacks along with three of my more specific patterns. Finding trends and patterns is the easy part. The devil is in the details.

PULLING IT ALL TOGETHER:
TRADING PULLBACKS IN TRENDING MARKETS

I believe "The Trend Is Your Friend" is the truest market adage. And, the best way to enter trends is on pullbacks. As seen in Figure 4.1, the precursors for trading pullbacks consist of a market in a strong trend (a) that has begun to correct (b). A trade (c) is triggered when the trend begins to resume and a protective stop is placed (d) should the trend not continue. As the trend persists, partial profits (e) should be taken and the stop on the remaining shares should be trailed higher (f). In a nutshell, this is my entire methodology.

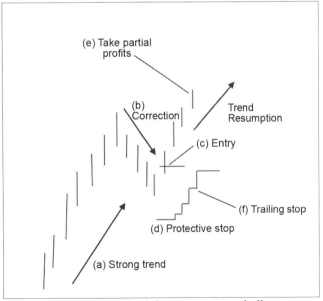

Figure 4.1~ My Methodology In A Nutshell

Let's break it down.

STRONG TREND

The market should be in a solid trend. Pullbacks can also occur in markets making an obvious trend transition (discussed in Section II). Trends can be gauged with Trend Qualifiers, moving averages or again, my favorite technique — simply looking at the chart and drawing an arrow in the direction of price movement.

WIDTH

The best stocks in strong trends usually do not consolidate for very long if they are to resume their move. Therefore, although I may occasionally make an exception, I generally ignore stocks after they pull back for more than 8 days. At this point, one has to wonder if the previous trend is slowing or coming to an end (Figure 4.2).

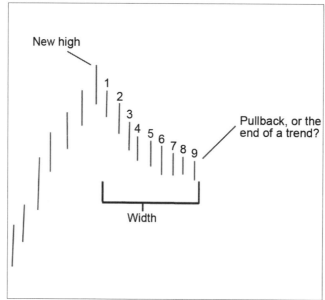

Figure 4.2 ~ Width of the Pullback

DEPTH

The depth (Figure 4.3) of corrections varies with the volatility of the stock and conditions of the market and representative sector. Volatile stocks can pull back deeply and still be in an uptrend. In longer term orderly bull markets, pullbacks are often shallow in nature. Conversely, in bear markets the pullback from the downtrend can be very sharp and vicious.

THE ENTRY

Waiting for an entry helps ensure that the market is moving in the anticipated direction. If an entry does not trigger, then the trade should be avoided. This technique of waiting for confirmation can keep you out of losing trades. The stock must move in the intended direction before taking a position. When buying stock this means that the stock is trading above the prior high. Again, this helps to ensure that the market has turned back in the direction of the longer-term momentum (Figure 4.4).

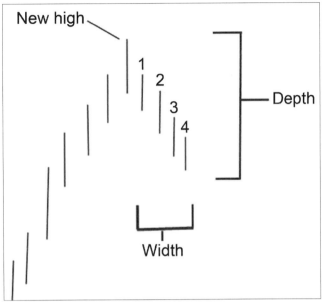

Figure 4.3 ~ Depth of the Pullback

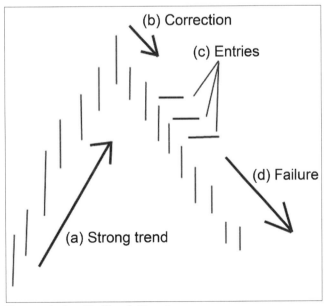

Figure 4.4 ~ Pullback Entries

In my first book, *Dave Landry on Swing Trading*, I stated that the entry point should be right above the high of the last bar of the pullback. When that book was written we were in the greatest bull market of the century. Referring to Figure 4.5, entering just above the high in a textbook fashion (a) or even early was the right thing to do since most trends resumed quickly. You had to get in before the train left the station. Today, stocks often fake out above the prior day's high and then sell off hard. It is possible that this is caused by market markers and savvy traders pushing the stock above the prior day's high in order to draw in, and subsequently take advantage of, traders looking to enter just above the prior day's high. It could also just be that the market is now very choppy, like it was after raging bull markets of the past. Considering the above, I have become more and more liberal with my entries. I often place them well above the prior day's high or above multiple highs. In other words, I like to give them some wiggle room (b).

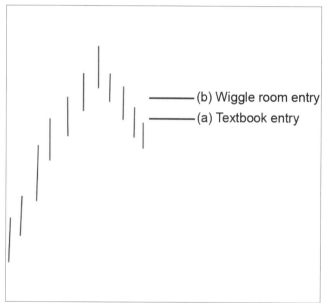

Figure 4.5 ~ Entry Volatility

The entry should be far enough away to help you avoid being triggered by noise alone (i.e. meaningless volatility). However, it should not be so far away that you give up too much of the trend. This is illustrated in Figure 4.6

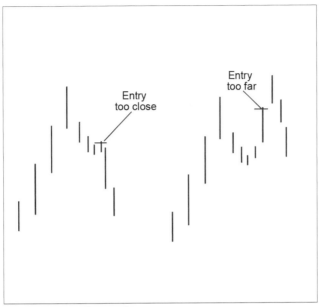

Figure 4.6 ~ Entry Proximity

The amount of room is arbitrary and depends on the price and volatility of the stock. It also depends on where the stock closed on the prior day. If a stock closed strongly, near its high, then you might want your entry further away to help ensure you do not get triggered on noise alone. If the stock closed poorly, near its low, the stock will have to travel a long distance in order to get past the prior day's high. Therefore, less wiggle room is needed. This is illustrated in Figure 4.7.

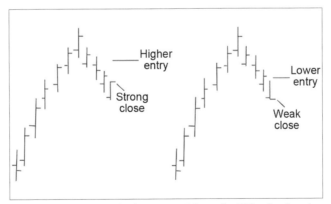

Figure 4.7 ~ Watch the Prior Close for Wiggle Guidance

As a general statement, over the last few years, I have found myself giving stocks more and more room on the entry. This has kept me out of a considerable amount of trades that would have resulted in a loss.

Let's take a look at one of my favorite examples.

In Figure 4.8 a prolonged downtrend in Hovnanian (HOV), a home builder, begins to form a double bottom and then rallies off the pattern. HOV pulls back briefly, forming a First Thrust (see chapter 9). The S&P 500 was in an uptrend and nearing all-time highs. The home builder stocks were also bottoming out and beginning to rally. All the pieces were coming together for a great trade.

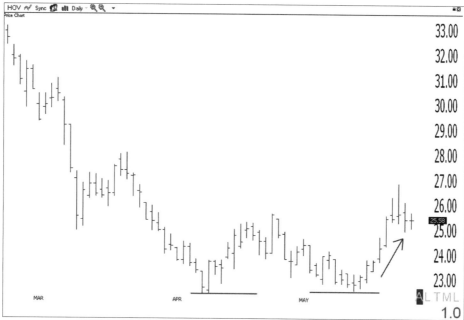

Figure 4.8 ~ HOV   *Chart Created With Telechart Platinum*

Now, let's look at potential entries in Figure 4.9. A textbook entry would go right above the high (a). A better entry would allow wiggle room (b). This is especially true since the current bar is an inside day, meaning the entire range is within the prior day's range.

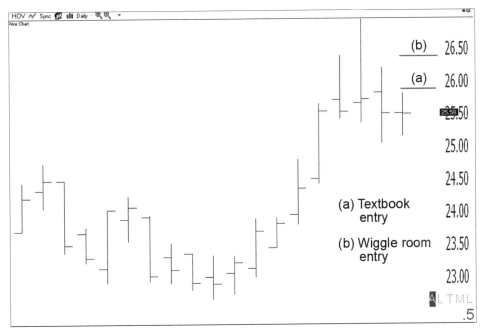

Figure 4.9 ~ HOV   Chart Created With Telechart Platinum

Now examine Figure 4.10 to see what happened. A textbook entry (a) would have triggered. But giving the stock some room (b) would have avoided a loss.

Figure 4.10 ~ HOV　　　　　　*Chart Created With Telechart Platinum*

As you can see, giving the stock wiggle room on the entry can help you avoid a losing trade. Keep in mind that in trading, there is always a trade off. The further you put your entry away the less likely you are to get triggered. However, if it does trigger, you will give up the extra wiggle in profits. It is like an insurance policy. You are paying a higher price to help avoid a false entry.

In good conditions, you might look to enter in more of a textbook manner. If conditions are great, you might even look to enter early. Otherwise, give the entry some wiggle room.

PROTECTIVE STOPS
Once the entry triggers, a protective stop should be placed to protect trading capital if the market does not cooperate. Keep in mind that on every trade there is the risk of loss. There-fore, stops must be used! Stop losses are a bit of a science and a bit of an art. There are no precise rules as to where they should be placed. Tight stops help to mitigate large losses, but they often guarantee that you will lose since they are likely to get hit on noise. By thinking they are keeping risk small, overly tight stops cause many people to lose money trading. Loose stops help ensure that you stay in a market long enough to capture a resumption of the trend. However, when the trend does not resume, the losses are larger.

In my first book I said that stops should go just below the pullback. Again, keep in mind that this was within the context of the raging bull market. As illustrated on the left side of Figure 4.11, stocks traded in more of an ideal fashion. Back then, it was a good idea to keep stops tight. Unfortunately, sans raging bull market, stocks take time to move and often have fits and starts. A stop placed precisely below the low of the pullback will often get hit. This can be frustrating as you then watch the stock take off without you. The reality of this post bull market trading is illustrated on the right side of Figure 4.11. Stops must be placed based on the volatility of the underlying asset. If a stock bounces around 5 points a day, the stop must be outside of that range. Otherwise, you will be taken out on volatility alone.

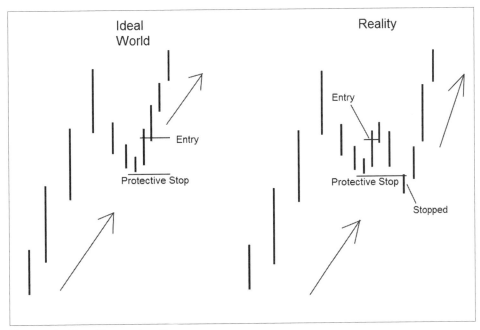

Figure 4.11 ~ Protective Stops

TAKING PARTIAL PROFITS

I like to exit half of my position for relatively small initial gains. Usually my first profit objective is an amount equal to the initial risk and then I move my stop to breakeven on the remainder of the position. Suppose I am risking $5 on a trade. When I have at least a $5 profit, I will exit half of my shares and then move my stop to breakeven — the price at which I entered the trade. The worst I can then do, barring overnight gaps, is to breakeven on the remaining shares. Should the trend continue longer term, this allows me to play with the market's money. This is how I am able to occasionally catch home runs from a shorter-term methodology.

Figure 4.12 illustrates the practice of taking partial profits at a level equal (b) to the entry price plus the initial risk (a) and that the stop should only be trailed higher once the initial profit target is hit (c). I did this to keep the concept of taking partial profits simple. In reality, you want to trail your stop higher if the stock moves in your favor even before the initial profit target is hit (refer back to figure 4.1).

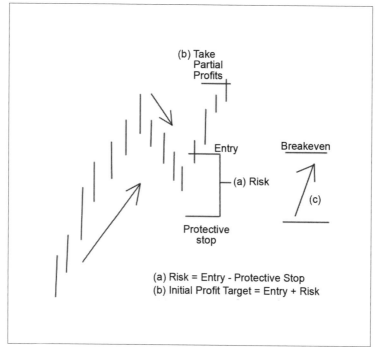

Figure 4.12 ~ Taking Partial Profits

TRAILING STOPS

Should the market continue to move in my favor, the protective stop is trailed higher so I do not give up too much of the trend when it reverses. Obviously "too much" is somewhat arbitrary and would depend on the volatility of the stock. Like the initial protective stop, the looser you are willing to trail, the better your chances of capturing a bigger move. However, you will lose more open profits when there is finally a reversal. I loosen the trailing stop as the position moves progressively in my favor. Suppose my initial stop is $5. Once I have $7 or $8 of open profits, I might loosen my trailing stop to $6. As the stock continues to move in my favor, I might loosen the stop even further. This increases the chances of me being able to participate in a longer-term move. The gradual loosening of trailing stops in attempt to ride out a longer-term winner is illustrated in Figure 4.13.

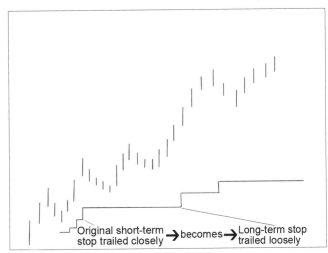

Figure 4.13 ~ Trailing Stops

SUMMARY

Successfully trading pullbacks starts with the process of identifying a stock in a strong trend that has recently corrected. You look to enter only if the trend shows signs of resuming. This can often help you avoid a losing trade. Once a position has been established, a protective stop is used just in case you are wrong. If the position moves in your favor, partial profits are taken and a stop is trailed higher. This is how you manage a short-term trade and hopefully have it turn into a longer-term winner.

CHAPTER 5
Managing Profits And Losses

To make money, you must first not lose money. Everyone wants to learn about trades that have the potential to capture large gains. No one wants to discuss what to do when they don't. Money management is not sexy. In fact, it is really boring.

In my first books, I put money management where it belongs — up front. Those books were geared more towards those with some trading knowledge. Assuming they had made some actual trades, and knowing traders are often pattern junkies, I figured they would be quick to move to the setup chapters. Money management would have a much better chance of getting read if I covered it early on.

Since I thought you would probably want to know how to make money before I showed you how to protect it, this time around I put the topic a little further into the book. I can assure you that this is the most important chapter in this text. Without a money management plan, money spent on this book, or any other book on trading, will have been wasted.

MANAGING LOSSES: WHY TRADING IS UNFAIR

Those new to trading think that if you lose 10 percent, you have to make 10 percent to get back to breakeven. Unfortunately, this is not true. In order to make back a 10 percent loss, you must earn at least 11.11 percent on your remaining equity. Even worse is that as losses deepen, the recovery percentage begins to grow geometrically. Those who have lost over 50 percent of their portfolio in the average mutual fund in 2008 quickly came to this painful realization. They have to make 100 percent on their remaining portfolio just to return to breakeven. This percent to recover is illustrated in Figure 5.1.

Percent Loss Of Capital	*Percent Gain Required To Recoup Losses*
10%	11.00%
20%	25.00%
30%	42.85%
40%	66.66%
50%	100.00%
60%	150.00%
70%	233.00%
80%	400.00%
90%	900.00%
100%	BROKE

Figure 5.1 ~ Gains Required To Recover Losses

Notice that as losses increase, the percent gain necessary to recover to breakeven increases at a much faster rate.

The geometric aspect is much better illustrated in a graph (Figure 5.2). Notice that the percent to recover grows at an accelerated rate as the percent loss increases. This illustrates the difficulty of recovering from losses and why money management is so important.

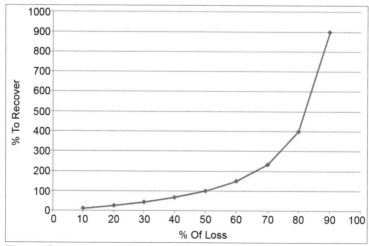

Figure 5.2 ~ Percent To Recover Losses

The amount of money lost while trading is known as drawdown. It is expressed as a percentage of your total trading equity. If all your trades were profitable, you would never experience a drawdown. Drawdown does not measure overall performance, only the money lost while achieving that performance. Its calculation begins only with a losing trade and continues as long as the account hits new equity lows.

Keep in mind that no matter how much you are up in your account at any given time — 100, 200, 300, or even 1000 percent — a 100 percent drawdown will wipe you out. Recovering from a drawdown can be extremely difficult and illustrates why money management is so important and why trading is unfair.

THE 1-2 PERCENT RULE

Risk no more than 1 percent to a maximum of 2 percent per trade based on stop placement. Therefore, on a $100,000 portfolio, you should only risk $1,000 (1 percent) to a maximum of $2,000 (2 percent) per trade if stopped out. Notice that I said "if stopped out." You are not "investing" $1,000 to $2,000 in a stock. You are taking a position and if it works, you will stay with the stock, look to take partial profits, and trail your stop. If it does not work, then you will exit if the stop is hit, no questions asked.

Considering the rule, suppose you have studied the price movement and volatility of a stock you would like to buy. You determine that it will require a $5 stop. For every 100 shares you buy, you are risking $500, regardless of the price of the equity. So, if you were to risk 1 percent of a $100,000 portfolio, you would buy 200 shares. Here is the math: amount risked = $100,000 * 1 percent = $1,000. 1,000 / 5 = 200 shares. Again, this does not mean that you buy $1,000 worth of stock. It means that if stopped out, barring overnight gaps, you will lose no more than 1 percent of your trading account or $1,000.

Notice above that I said "barring overnight gaps." Just because you are only willing to risk 1 percent, does not mean that is all that is at stake. A news event can occur that could cause the stock to open significantly lower than it closed the prior day. Sooner or later you will get hit for much more than you intended to risk. This is yet another factor why it is important to keep position sizes reasonable.

THE ART OF PLACING PROTECTIVE STOPS

As I have said throughout this book, every trade, no matter how well thought out, has the potential to turn into a loser. Therefore, you must place stops on all trades. Stops are a bit of a science and a bit of an art. Tight stops help to mitigate large losses but they almost guarantee that you will frequently lose money since they are likely to get hit on normal market fluctuations. And, ironically, many who think they are keeping risk in check with tight stops are in fact creating more losses for themselves. Loose stops help to ensure you stay in a market long enough to capture a resumption of the trend. However, when the trend does not resume, the losses are larger — unless, obviously, the trader compensates by trading fewer shares.

Now let's discuss the Goldilocks nature of setting stops.

THIS STOP IS TOO TIGHT

In an ideal world, a tight stop could be placed right below the low of the pullback as inferred in Figure 5.3. Unfortunately, very seldom does a market do exactly as we desire. Markets often continue in the obvious direction, but not without trading back and forth first. Therefore, a tight stop would likely be hit on this normal market volatility alone. This can be frustrating as you watch a stock take off without you. This is illustrated in the right side of Figure 5.3.

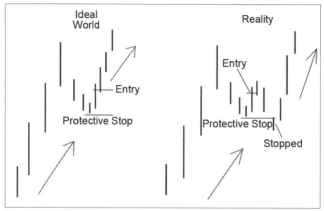

Figure 5.3 ~ Very Tight Stop

THIS STOP IS TOO LOOSE

Loose stops help to ensure you stay in a market long enough to capture a resumption of the trend. However, when the trend does not resume, too much is given up. The trend is obviously not reasserting and you should have exited long before it reached this point. This is illustrated in Figure 5.4.

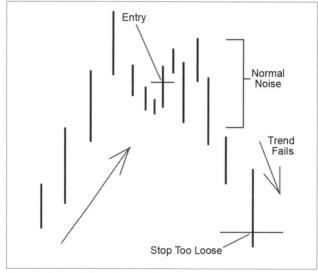

Figure 5.4 ~ Very Loose Stop

THIS STOP IS JUST RIGHT

The ideal stop would be far enough away to just barely survive normal noise but not so far as to keep the position open when the trend has obviously reversed (Figure 5.5). You are probably wondering how to define normal noise? Unfortunately, no one knows exactly how far a market will go before resuming its trend, or if it will even resume the trend at all. Normal noise can seem somewhat arbitrary. Statistical measurements such as average true range or historical volatility tell us how much the stock has fluctuated and will likely continue to fluctuate, all things constant. "All things constant" is the key phrase in that sentence. In markets, things seldom remain constant. Statistical measurements can often be quite large — outside of what one would ever consider using for a protective stop. Additionally, markets do not trade in a purely statistical fashion. If they did, statisticians would own the world.

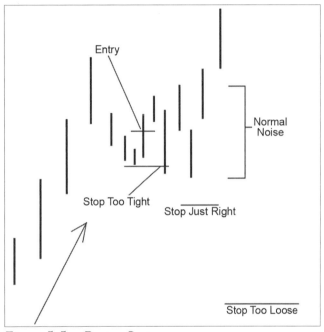

Figure 5.5 ~ Proper Stop

So what is a trader to do? The good news is that it does not have to be complicated. Common sense is your best ally when placing stops. Simply look at the charts and notice how much a stock moves on a daily basis. If a stock moves $5 to $10 a day, you obviously cannot use a $1 or $2 stop. Otherwise, you are almost guaranteed to be stopped out on noise.

Your own trading can be a good gauge for where to place stops. If you are constantly getting stopped out right before markets make a big move, then your stops are probably too tight. I have worked with many traders who have done just this. All that stood between them and becoming profitable was to loosen their stops a bit. This can be counter intuitive for many, especially since tight stops seem to be universally preached. Eyeball the market and see how much it bounces around. Then, put your stop outside of that range.

Keep in mind that if a market does require a fairly loose stop, you need to compensate for risk by trading fewer shares or contracts. This way, the percentage loss to the portfolio would remain minimal. Again, you do not want to risk more than 1 to 2 percent per position if the stop is hit. Regardless of where the stop is placed, the losses should be minimal if they occur.

SOMETIMES YOUR BEST DEFENSE IS A GOOD OFFENSE

If your stops are outside of normal volatility, but you are still getting stopped out repeatedly, then it might not be your stops. It could be your stock picking. Make sure you are trading the best of the best setups. Make sure that the sector and the market confirm your opinion. Look at other stocks within the sector to see if there are some that would better candidates. Study prior winners. The better you get at stock picking, the less you will get stopped out. Defense is crucial but a good offense will keep you out of mediocre trades to begin with.

MANAGING PROFITS: PLAYING WITH THE MARKET'S MONEY USING TRAILING STOPS

Here is the fun part. When the trend does resume, we get to manage our profits. By trailing a protective stop higher and taking partial profits when offered, we take money out of the market and position ourselves for long-term gains.

Let's look at how to do this.

As the market moves in our favor, we trail our stops higher (or lower for shorts). We hope to stay with the position long enough to take initial profits. We want to continue to stay with the position as long as it moves in our favor. How long? As long as the stock moves in my favor, hopefully at least 10 years.

Revisiting the partial profits example (Figure 5.6), your risk (a) is the distance to from the entry to the protective stop. Adding that distance to the entry gives us our initial profit target (b). Once the initial profit target is hit, we exit half of our shares and then immediately move the stop on the remainder to breakeven (c).

The Figure was designed to illustrate risk and the taking of partial profits. You actually would also want to trail your stop higher as the position moves in your favor, even if the initial profit target is not hit yet.

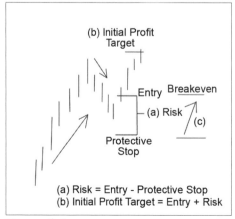

Figure 5.6

Let's break this down bar by bar in Figure 5.7. Suppose the stock triggers and closes the day nicely in your favor. You would then raise your protective stop by that amount (1). Your initial protective stop becomes a trailing stop. You trail it behind the price.

The following day the stock continues to rally out of the pullback. We then raise the trailing stop by that amount (2).

On day 3 our trade closes higher once again. We then raise the stop by that amount (3).

On day 4, the initial profit target is hit. In fact, the stock actually opens above the profit target, offering us more than we were initially looking for. We exit half of our shares and move the stop to breakeven on the remainder (4).

Now, barring overnight gaps lower, the worst we can do is breakeven on the balance of the position. This is a great place to be from both a psychological and financial standpoint. We are now able to "play with the market's money."

Trailing stops are only moved higher if the market moves in your favor. If the stock does not close at a new high since you entered, you leave the stop where it is.

On day 5 the stock drops fairly sharply. Since this is an unfavorable move, there is nothing to do with the trailing stop. You simply leave it where it is (5).

In order for us to raise the trailing stop again, the stock must make a new closing high. Because the stock closed below the initial profit target on the day we took profits, it must also close above the initial profit target before we trail the stop further. This sounds more complicated than it really is. Essentially, if our initial risk and profit target was $5, we trail the stop no closer than $5 below the close. If the stock closes more than $5 above the trailing stop, we raise the trailing stop to $5 below the close.

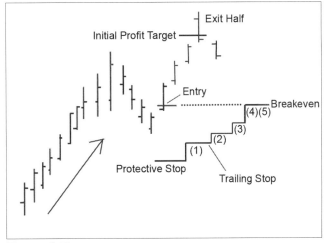

Figure 5.7

On day 6 (Figure 5.8), the stock begins to rally again. But since it does not close above the initial profit target and at a new closing high, we once again leave the trailing stop where it is.

On day 7, the stock continues nicely higher. This time, it closes above the initial profit target and at a new closing high. We once again trail our stop higher (7). We are now in a fantastic position. Since our trailing stop is now above our entry, the worst we can now do is a profit on the remainder of the position (barring overnight gaps).

Now that the remaining half of our position is at a profit, we have the luxury of trailing our stops even more loosely. This will help us to participate in a longer-term uptrend. Notice on day 8, the stock makes a significant move higher but we only ratchet our stop slightly higher.

As the stock continues higher, we continue to trail more loosely (9). This is how we turn a short-term trade with tight risk control into a longer-term winner.

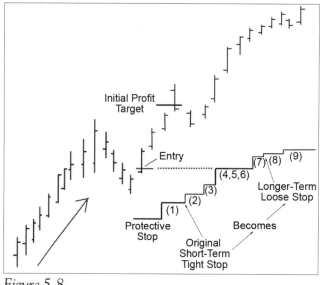

Figure 5.8

SUMMARY

Trading is unfair. Percentage wise you have to make back more than you lose in order to get back to breakeven. What is worst is, that as the losses mount, the percent needed to break-even grows geometrically. Since there is a risk of loss on every trade, protective stops must be used.

Placement of stops is as much art as science. Loose stops help you to capture longer-term trends but you give up too much of that trend when it reverses. Tight stops help to mitigate the amount lost but almost guarantee you a loss on many trades. The ideal stop is placed just outside of the normal noise. Normal noise is somewhat arbitrary, but simply looking at the chart will give you a good idea of where it should be. If a stock moves in your favor, trail the stop higher and take partial profits when offered. On an extended move, you can trail your stop loosely. This is how you get the best of both worlds, getting both a short-term gain and a longer-term winner.

CHAPTER 6
Trader Psychology

"Baseball is 90% mental. The other half is physical."
— Yogi Berra

I was fortunate enough to have Julie Manz, a psychologist who actually trades for a living, help me organize this book. Knowing the emotions involved of making and losing money, we were not sure exactly where to place Trader Psychology. It is a chicken versus the egg thing. You have to understand the psychology of trading to trade but you have to trade to understand the psychology of trading. We agreed that some of the psychology might be a little heavy for the first steps. However, we also agreed that they were very crucial for the beginner to know. Therefore, if you are new to trading, some of the following might not make a whole lot of sense. I can assure you though, after just a few trades, it will.

TRADING PSYCHOLOGY

We have now come to the most difficult part of trading. You are the biggest obstacle to becoming a successful trader. Why? Trading will put demands on you that you have never imagined. Markets will frustrate you, forcing you to give up right before they make a big move. On the flip side, markets can often be totally accommodating and will lull you into a false sense of security. Further, the market often rewards bad behavior and can be the worst teacher.

Sometimes the more you try to make something happen, the less the market will cooperate. Other times, the market will reward you when you are not doing anything. It is a business filled with paradoxes.

The good news is that if you can conquer your own emotions, then you can use the charts to help understand the psychology of the masses. You will learn that what is, is. You will have the discipline to execute your plan without any personal bias. You will accept the fact that you could be wrong, but know that longer term you will be right. You will know that you might lose a few battles, but not the war.

Although my methodology is simple, I never said that trading was easy. However, if you are willing to work hard to understand the charts, and more importantly yourself, you will be successful.

I HAVE NEVER MET AN UNSUCCESSFUL PAPER TRADER

When learning to trade, I suggest that you paper trade for a while until you have a feel for the methodology. Be warned though, I have never met an unsuccessful paper trader. You will tend to do what is right. You see opportunities clearly, follow your plan, and your virtual account will grow and grow.

Once real money is on the line things will change. A loss will be equated to a mortgage payment. And, a string of lost mortgage payments will make it tough for you to execute your plan, knowing that the potential exists for you to lose yet another one.

How do you move from a success in the paper world to a success in the real world? Simple, trade at a very small size and slowly build as you gain confidence in the methodology and more importantly, yourself.

THE 3 M's TO TRADING PSYCHOLOGY

There are three aspects to trading psychology: Money Management, Methodology, and Mind. Proper money management will help you keep your losses and more importantly, your feelings associated with those losses in check. It will also keep you in the game for the long term. Understanding your methodology will keep you from becoming too euphoric when things are going well and keep you from becoming too despondent when they are not. In dull markets, it will put you at ease, knowing that sometimes the best action is no action. Controlling your emotions will prevent you from trying to impose your will on the market.

MONEY MANAGEMENT

MONEY MANAGEMENT WILL CURE A MULTITUDE OF SINS

If you respect risk and trade at a small size, then any single loss or the inevitable string of losses should not have a material impact on your account or your psyche. As "location, location, location" is to real estate, "money management, money management, money management" is to trading.

LONGEVITY IS KEY

In bull markets, stocks go up. In bear markets, stocks go down. And in choppy markets, stocks go sideways. If you are willing to take my word for it, you will do great. You simply overlay the arrows from Chapter 3 onto your charts to determine trend. You ignore your personal biases and extraneous information. If you can do this, then you can greatly compress the amount of time it will take you to become successful. For 99 percent of the rest of you, you will have to make your own mistakes to learn.

You will have to fight trends, try to make something happen in dull markets, bail out for tiny profits on soon to become big winners, and give up right before the next great bull (or bear) market. You will have to get burned by listening to know it all gurus or "insiders." You will have to average down only to compound your losses. The list goes on and on. I have identified all of these pitfalls in this book. However, me telling you not to do these things and you not doing them are two different things. The good news is that unless you are extremely obstinate, then you will eventually get it. So how do you survive until you get it? Simple, money management, money management, money management.

HONOR YOUR STOP

Why is it so hard to honor your stops? It is because we are taught not to quit in life. In trading, quitting is often the thing to do. If you are new to trading or lack discipline, you must place actual stops. You cannot say that you will exit the market if it goes against you by X amount and then sit there like a deer in the headlights as the market blows past that stop.

Placing actual stops makes your decision a passive one and not an active one. The market will make the decision for you if you are wrong.

Once you gain experience, confidence and discipline, you can use mental stops to help avoid being stopped out under certain specific conditions (see Chapter 15 Advanced Discretionary Techniques). However, when learning or having difficulties following your plan, you should place actual stops.

VIEW A POTENTIAL LOSS AS A COST

There is a cost to doing business in any field. You will have to pay for office supplies, computers, printers, and inventory if you are selling something tangible. When you run low on supplies or inventory, you accept the fact that you have to buy more. A loss in trading must be viewed the same way. It is simply the cost of doing business.

WITH VOLATILITY COMES OPPORTUNITY

More volatile stocks, within reason, tend to offer the best opportunities. They have made huge moves in the past and have the potential to make huge moves in the future. However, since they do move around a lot, they require a wider stop. In order to keep risk in line, you must trade fewer shares than you would on a less volatile stock.

It amazes me that people will not take a trade because it requires a fairly wide stop. They tell me, "Oh, the percentage is too high, I can't risk that many points." What they fail to realize is that if they are adjusting for the volatility by trading fewer shares, barring overnight gaps, their risks on the volatile stock should be no different than less volatile stocks in their portfolio.

Yes, it is true that the risk of something bad happening in a more volatile stock is there statistically. And, sooner or later you will get whacked in a volatile stock. However, since surprises usually happen in the direction of the trend, longer term, the big favorable moves should more than compensate for the occasional negative outlier. There is always a risk that something could go very wrong, even in less volatile stocks. This is not why these individuals are ignoring opportunities.

These traders are letting their ego get in the way of opportunity, using risk as an excuse. They simply cannot see themselves letting a market go against them by the amount that the market dictates. They would see themselves as a failure if this happened. Yet, this amount is normal noise alone. They blame risk, but if they are adhering to money management rules, then barring overnight gaps, the amount of money risked should be no different than any other trade. Forget about points risked, or percentage of price risk per trade, and view each trade as a small fixed risk of your account.

Learn From Your Losses

When I suffer a setback, I do not think of myself as losing, I am simply learning how to win.
— Ted Turner

Success is going from failure to failure without losing your enthusiasm.
— Abraham Lincoln

My wife Marcy calls me "Hobby Boy." If I am not in front of my screens working, I am into something, and not just casually. I rarely sit still. I spend 60-70 hours sitting in front of my computers each week, so the last thing I want to do is sit still. One of my hobbies is flying high-powered rockets. One of the guys in our club crashes a lot of them. A friend of mine remarked, "Andrew sure does crash a lot of rockets." The thing is, he also flies a lot of rockets. He travels the nation attending many launches. He has achieved what few in the sport have. There is a saying in rocketry, usually said in a strong Forrest Gump accent: "If you ain't crashin' rockets, you ain't flying any." Another common saying is "you don't learn nothing from a successful flight" (We are "rocket scientists" not English majors).

Although I firmly believe trading is not rocket science, if you ain't taking losses, you ain't trading. The more you trade, the more likely you are to have losses. Good traders make a lot of money, but they also lose a lot too. They know that losses are part of the game.

You must learn from your losses. If you did everything right and you still lose on a trade, then pat yourself on the back for doing the right thing, knowing that consistently doing the right thing will pay off in the long run. If you did something that you should not have done and created a large loss, then learn from it! Whenever I screw up in a big way, Marcy tells me, "Well, you will do that once!" If I do the same thing again, I am haunted by her voice.

The Market Will Always Be There, Will You?
I have a bad habit of beating a dead horse. It drives Marcy and especially my daughters nuts. Whenever they say, "Come'on dad, you can't beat a dead horse!" I always tell them, "You can flatten it!" By now, you have probably realized that my "dead horse" is money management.

Again, keep risks in line. As mentioned previously, it is a business of longevity. By keeping losses small, you will learn from them until you become successful.

The Highs Are High And The Lows Are Low
Balance is key. You must learn to control your emotions. You cannot get too excited when things are going well nor can you get too depressed when things are not.

Once again, it all boils down to money management. By keeping positions small, a loss, or the inevitable string of losses, should not bother you too much. You should be able to move on, continue to do your analysis without bias, and then execute your plan, knowing that you will succeed longer term.

On the flip side, gains should not get you too elated. If you did your homework, practiced proper money management, and executed your plan without forcing your will onto the market, then it is okay to feel good about successful trades. You cannot let a string of winners go to your head and become reckless. Yet again, money management rears its ugly head. By keeping positions in line, you will be able to control the emotional highs and the emotional lows.

METHODOLOGY

KNOW YOUR METHODOLOGY

Knowing your methodology will go a long way in helping you combat the psychological issues of trading. If you understand the nuances then you will not get too despondent when things are not going well, and you will not get too euphoric when things are great. I cannot speak for other methodologies, but I can tell you some nuances of mine. Swing to intermediate-term trading can be skewed, streaky, and depends on the market to persist in its trend. Let's explore these further.

Skewed: The majority of gains come from the minority of positions. The occasional big winners are key. Without these few big winners, results are mediocre at best. This is not easy for many. Taking nine losing trades and ignoring the tenth, which would have made back all the money, and then some, can be quite frustrating.

Streaky: The majority of profits will often come over short periods of time. Markets often make large gains quickly and then they tend to consolidate. If you are not participating during these times your performance will be less than average.

THE MARKET MUST TREND AND PERSIST IN THAT TREND

Obviously, a trend following methodology requires the market to trend. Yes, the trend is your friend, but only until it ends. Sharp reversals from established trends can and do occur. During these times you will experience a drawdown. Hopefully though, you will get stopped out at only modest losses on your positions and a new trend will emerge in the opposite direction, creating new opportunities. Choppy markets are detrimental to the methodology. The good news is, after getting chewed up a bit, the market will present fewer and fewer setups. It is self regulating. If the market remains trendless for extended periods, you will likely find yourself completely shut out and patiently waiting for the next opportunity. This of course, is provided that you are disciplined enough not to try to make something happen when opportunity does not exist.

There are no perfect methodologies that will lead to eternal profitability without losses along the way. If there were, someone would have exploited this and there would no longer be a market. As imperfect as my methodology is, it is the best thing I have found after two decades of searching. Markets will trend. In the 1600s it was tulips in the Netherlands and rice in Japan. In more recent times, there have been huge runs and subsequent falls in Internet, energy, and real estate stocks to name a few. And, they will trend in the future. Prices will rise and prices will fall. This is one thing about markets that I can guarantee.

An Edge, Not An Assurance

Any given trade, no matter how well thought out, has the potential to become a losing trade. As I discussed in Chapter 1, unless you are all knowing, you cannot possibly know all the new variables that will enter the market after you. Knowing this going in should make handling that loss easier.

You Must Be Present To Win

Because trend following is skewed and streaky, you never know when the next big trend will come along. Without that trend, your performance will be mediocre at best. It amazes me that people will take June through August off because the market "does not trend during the summer." True, as a general statement, the market can be choppy with low volume. However, large trends can occur in all months of the year, even during summer.

Being present to win does not mean sitting in front of a screen all day watching every tick. It means that you must do your homework nightly even in less-than-ideal conditions.

Instant Success Can Be More Detrimental Than Failure

This is yet another paradox of trading. A friend of mine, Joe Corona, has been trading for his entire adult life. He travels the world looking for opportunities. A few years ago, he decided to set up shop in India. His traders came from modest backgrounds. They really needed the job.

Joe once told me, "Dave, I like to see the new guys have their ass handed to them right away. This way, and only this way, do they learn to respect risk." For fear of losing their job, these traders quickly learn to do the right thing. While others who experience instant success have no idea what hit them when the inevitable first drawdown comes along.

The World's Worst Teacher

The market often rewards bad behavior. You exit a stock because your stop is hit. You are okay with this because you followed your plan. The market then immediately reverses. You begin to think, "If only I stayed with the position." The next time the market goes against you, you decide you are not going to get tricked again. This time though, the market does not reverse and what started out as a small manageable loss is now huge.

The market will give you loss after loss forcing you to abandon a methodology right before it takes off without you. On the flip side, the market will lull you into a false sense of confidence. You trade larger and larger, taking on excessive risk. You print money until your risks become so excessive that one or two bad trades wipe you out.

Learn from the market, but realize that sometimes it can be a lousy instructor.

The Waiting Is The Hardest Part

Tom Petty got it right. The waiting is the hardest part. Trading is an active verb. However, the irony is that there are many times when you should not be doing anything. Doing nothing is difficult if not impossible for most. Yet, it is exactly what you should be doing during these times, nothing.

In dull, choppy markets I often preach that we are more wait-ers than trade-ers. This is another snag for successful people. More than likely, prior success in life came from action. In trading, we often find that the best thing to do is nothing unless there is something to do.

Jesse Livermore, one of the greatest traders of all time, said it best, "Remember this: When you are doing nothing, those speculators who feel they must trade day in and day out, are laying the foundation for your next venture. You will reap benefits from their mistakes." The next time the market becomes choppy, write that quote on a Post-It and stick it to your monitor.

Trade The Best And Leave The Rest

As I said earlier, if you are reading this book, there is a good chance that you are smart. You are probably also motivated and successful. Therefore, I think it is fairly safe to say that you want the best in life.

It is amazing that the same people who want the best in life will deal with mediocrity in the markets. In some of the best markets, I will get asked for an opinion on some of the worst stocks. The market will be in an obvious trend, the sector will be in an obvious trend, and most stocks within the sector will be in obvious trends. Yet, I get asked for an opinion on stocks that are going sideways. Here is my all-time favorite example.

In June of 2002, the S&P was in an obvious downtrend. In fact, it is set up as a pullback from lows. The Biotech sector and Nasdaq Biotech iShares were also in a solid downtrend and set up as a pullback from lows. With the market and sector in an obvious downtrend and both setup as a pullbacks, there were numerous stocks within the sector that were also trending lower and set up. Yet, I got asked by someone who claims to be a fellow card carrying trend following moron for an opinion on Gilead Sciences (GILD), a stock he was considering. The stock was all over the place. The best that could be said about GILD was that it had been trading sideways for months (Figure 6.1).

I am not sure why someone who considers themselves a trend trader would pick this wide and loose stock when so many others are trending. In fact, since the sector itself was set up, and he could have simply traded that via an Exchange Traded Fund.

Figure 6.1 ~ GILD   *Chart Created With Telechart Platinum*

MICROMANAGEMENT IN A MICROWAVE SOCIETY

Suppose you did your homework and found a stock to buy. It is in a solid trend and is set up nicely. The market, the sector, and even most of the stocks within the sector are all trending. All the pieces are coming together. You know where you are going to enter, place your protective stop, where you will take partial profits, and how you will trail your stop. You have left nothing to chance. You have a plan.

The stock opens, triggers and you enter. So far, so good. You are following your plan. However, a few minutes later the stock begins to slide. You begin to stress and think that you should take the loss before it gets any larger. You exit. You then watch in anguish over the next days and weeks as the stock skyrockets without you.

Admittedly, my methodology is not like Ron Popeil's Showtime 6000 Rotisserie where you "set it and forget it." You will have to take some action after you enter a trade (by trailing stops). For the most part though, you will have to give things time to work. As long as you have done your homework, then stick with your positions, good, bad, or indifferent. Obsess before you enter a trade, not afterwards.

THE RIP VAN WINKLE TEST

Are current market conditions not favorable for your methodology? For trend following, this means that the market has been trading sideways. Next to drawing an arrow, a simple way to determine that a market has traded sideways is to look at where it closed today vs. where it closed a week ago, a month ago, and several months ago. I have dubbed this the Rip Van Winkle "Sleep Test." Imagine looking at the stock indices in a newspaper and going to sleep for a few weeks or months. Now imagine that you wake up and check the newspaper. If it has not changed much during this period, then it is not trending. And guess what? Just like you cannot get a tan when the sun is not shining, a trend following methodology does not work when there is not a trend.

Live In The Now
People will often ask me where I think the market will be six months or even a year or more from now. My answer is always the same, "I have no freaking idea." And, neither do you, or anyone else for that matter. Just because no one knows where the market will be months or years from now, does not mean you cannot profit from trading.

As previously mentioned, the market can do three things: go up, go down, or go sideways. If it has been doing one of those things for months, then the chances are that it will continue to do that, at least over the short term. Our job is to predict the short term, get it right and hopefully stay around while a longer-term trend develops. You cannot trade off the left side of your chart and you do not know what will happen in the distant future. All you can do is live in the now.

You Have To Be Willing To Take A Little Heat
Every now and then, you will enter a trade and it will instantly move in your favor and continue. The initial profit target will be hit with ease. The stock will continue to trend in your favor as you relax and trail your stop higher to ride out a big winner. The other 99 percent of the time the trade will move against you, at least initially. Therefore you have to be willing to take a little heat. Your protective stop must be outside of the normal volatility of the market. You have to be prepared to have the stock go against you by at least the amount of the normal volatility. If a stock bounces around $5 a day, you can not stress out if it moves a few dollars against you.

Be Careful Not To Get Too Close To The Markets
Some of my biggest gains have come when I was away from my computer. This was especially true early in my career when I used to watch a screen way too much. My most memorable lesson occurred during a sailing trip in the West Indies. I wanted to shut down my portfolio before I left so I could focus on relaxing, but I decided to leave a few of the most promising positions on. When I got back to the United States, I grabbed a newspaper in the airport to check on my positions. Alright! I then announced to the crew that I had just paid for my trip and then some. When I got back to the office, I closed all positions and patted myself on the back. I watched in agony over the next few weeks as my former positions continued to run. I would have made many times the amount if I would have just stayed on vacation.

When people have success in trading while juggling a full-time career, they assume that they will automatically be even more successful once they can focus exclusively on trading full time. Unfortunately, many times this is not the case. Watching a screen all day for a longer-term methodology can be damaging to both your financial and psychological health. Every little tick becomes larger than life. It will look like a new trend is emerging or an old one is ending. You will find yourself firing off day trades, micromanaging yourself out of soon-to-become big winners, and taking setups that are mediocre at best. Sitting in front of a screen all day is like sitting in front of a slot machine.

Busy traders make good traders. They tend to trade only when opportunities present themselves and then they go off to save lives, build buildings, and do other great things. If you do have the luxury of being able to watch the markets all day, make sure you have some other interest to keep you busy. Do not depend on the market for entertainment. In dull conditions, do some research or study historical markets, enjoy a hobby, start a new business, or pay some attention to your friends and loved ones.

THE MARKET DOES NOT CARE ABOUT YOUR COMFORT ZONE

Many newer traders quit trading when market volatility increases. Yet, if you are a short-to-intermediate-term trader, volatility is your friend. Some of your best trades will come when the market seems the scariest.

PEOPLE PLAN THEIR LIVES BUT NOT THEIR TRADES

Suppose you are going to take a vacation. Unless you are going to be like Kwai Chang Caine and just wander around the American West, there is a good chance that you have done some planning. You know where you are going. You have gassed up the car or booked your flights. You probably have a hotel reserved or at least know that there are plenty of vacancies in the area. True, you may be a little more adventurous and leave some things to chance, but in general, you have a plan. You know when you are leaving, what you are going to do while you are there, and when you are coming back.

It is safe to say that most people plan their lives. Yet, in trading, most do not. They do not have a clue about where they are getting in, where they are getting out, and how much they are going to risk. It is amazing that they trade without a plan even though this can be much more expensive, and certainly much less fun than the aforementioned vacation.

Plan your trade and trade your plan. Know how much you will risk. Know where you will take partial profits. Know where you will exit if you are wrong. When things are going well, you will be able to see what you are doing right. And more importantly, when things are not you will be able to easily see what you are doing wrong.

GOOD TIMES FOLLOW BAD: AFRICAN QUEEN SYNDROME

When I was a young child, we often went to my grandmother's house on Sundays. We had steak fried in a cast iron skillet for lunch and ice cream sandwiches for desert — as many as we could sneak without getting caught. There always seemed to be a classic movie on television. One of the few that I remember was the "African Queen."

I was enthralled by the trials of Charlie and Rose as they tried to escape the enemy. I remember cheering for them as they dodged bullets, ran rapids, and fought off leeches. If only they could make it to the lake at the bottom of the river, they would be home free. Exhausted, defeated, and deflated, they gave up. The camera panned back for one of the most powerful scenes in cinema. They were a few feet from reaching the lake.

By now, you may be wondering what does the African Queen have to do with trading? It is simple. Time and time again, I see people give up in less than ideal conditions right before the next trend. If only they could have held on for just a little while longer. As one client told me, "I feel like I broke up with my fiancé and the next Saturday she won the lottery."

Bad Times Follow Good: Beware Of The Permanent Market Hypothesis
Why do the majority of people who win the lottery end up worse off or even bankrupt within five years? The reason is that they become what is known as "lottery rich." The money comes fast and easy. They assume that the money will always be there. Economists refer to this as the permanent income hypothesis.

Markets are no different. When conditions are good people assume that their methodology will always work. They gain confidence and begin risking more and more. I have seen people sell puts (a bullish option strategy where the profits are limited but risks are virtually unlimited) in bull markets and make huge gains, only to give it all up the first time a bear market comes along. I have seen people do extremely well buying oversold markets and selling overbought markets until the next trend comes long and wipes them out. The list of very brilliant, but brief careers goes on and on.

All methodologies have a sweet spot. They do exceptionally well for a while then underperform. As we say in the south, "the sun does not shine on the same dog's buttocks every day." Do not assume that great market conditions will last forever. You must experience a variety of conditions. If you only bought stocks in a bull market, then you will not know what hit you when the next bear market comes along. If you have only traded a market that is trending, then you will become very anxious when you experience a choppy market or a sharp reversal.

Enjoy great conditions but realize that they will not last forever. Do not modify the methodology when an unfavorable market environment appears. If you do, you will end up being perpetually out of phase, quitting right before the plan begins working. I have many clients who stay with me for a brief period, go off to chase rainbows, and then return five and even ten years later. These are some of my favorite people because they have learned that there are no perfect methods and a simple trend following approach can work.

The Market Does Not Know Or Care That You Are In
It amazes me that people will buy a volatile stock and then stress out when it continues to be volatile. They get anxious when a stock that has been bouncing up and down $5 a day or more has gone even $1 against them. For some reason, they think that because they are in the stock, it will somehow only behave in a way that is only favorable to them.

"But Dave, I thought the trend was your friend? And, that by following your methodology you will be successful?" Yes, longer term, I believe these things. Shorter term, I know that prices will fluctuate. I also know that I can and often will be wrong. The approach that I am suggesting is not perfect. Remember, no methods are. There will be a chance of loss on each and every trade. That goes for every methodology. Since no knows exactly where a market is headed, the market does not know or care that you are in for the ride.

MAKING DECISIONS AND LIVING WITH THEM

Trading, like life, boils down to making decisions. That is the easy part. Living with them is hard. Making the decision to marry the most beautiful girl I have ever met was easy. Living with her is not. (Just kidding babe! I love yah.) Seriously, if you plan your trade and trade your plan, it will be much easier for you to live with your decisions.

IN THEORY, THEORY AND PRACTICE ARE THE SAME. IN PRACTICE, THEY ARE NOT.

In addition to market experience, you will need some psychological experience. You will need to experience a variety of conditions. You must know what happens in bull markets, what happens in bear markets, and what happens in choppy markets. Needing market experience is obvious. You will also need some psychological experience. If I told you that sooner or later a sharp market reversal will wipe out some, if not all of your open trades, you could pull up historical charts to know that I am serious. Knowing this can happen and actually getting wiped out on all your positions are two different things. You will frequently make a little and, unfortunately, lose a little more over and over for six to eight months (or occasionally even longer) before the next big trend develops. You could look at the charts to see that I am correct. However, until you get chewed up for months on end and give up in frustration right before the next trend, you will never know what it is really like to experience an extended choppy market. You will also need to experience a runaway momentum market. Nothing is quite like being euphoric about the prospect of waking up to see how much money you made overnight. Me telling you not to let this go to your head and it not happening are two different things.

IF and that is a big IF, you could follow everything outlined in this book, I firmly believe that, in time, you will become a successful trader. What stands between you and your success is putting the theory into practice while at the same time putting your emotions aside. I will bet that by now you get the concept that both good and bad things will occur. I hope that you will be able to live with the reality when it actually happens. You will have to experience it to see how you will react. Again, money management cures a multitude of sins. It will keep you in the game until you learn to conquer your emotions.

MIND

HANDLING LOSSES

Scientists have proven that when thinking of something, your body reacts as if it were reality. Try this yourself. Close your eyes and think of something that would make you very happy. Now pay attention to your body language. Do you feel relaxed? Now, do the opposite. Think about an uncomfortable situation. Do you feel anxious?

Mentally rehearsing can be a great tool for handling losing trades. Plan your trade and know exactly where your stop will be. Then, mentally take the loss before you enter. Do not think that you can simply handle this. Close your eyes and imagine the stop is hit and see how it makes you feel. If this causes you any anxiety then you are trading at too large of size. If you cannot handle the equivalent of another mortgage, car or charge card payment, reduce your size.

There Are Only Two Variables

There are only two variables in trading: you and the market. You cannot control the market. Trust me. Many, including governments, have tried with vast amounts of money. In fact, in 2008 the market dropped sharply after the US Treasury announced an $800 billion bailout. This was on top of previous multi-billion dollar subsidies, bringing the cost to well over a trillion dollars. Therefore, I think it is safe to say that NO ONE can control the markets. The only thing you can control is you.

Control Freaks Need Not Apply

Trading attracts the brightest minds. Therefore, it is likely that you have been successful in your current or prior career. Chances are that your success stems from your ability to control the situation. True, some things may have been left to chance, but for the most part, you being in control probably contributed greatly to your success. But, as we have just seen, no one is bigger than the markets. No one can control the markets, at least not for very long. Operating in an environment that cannot be controlled is difficult. You have to realize that the only thing that you can control is yourself.

Is It Me?

Not long after I quit my day job to become a trader, I began to get chewed up in the markets. Depressed, I wondered what was wrong with me. After all, I had done very well while I still had a job and I did have some initial success as a pro. I had hoped that a seminar would be just what the doctor ordered. Although I did learn a few tips and tricks from the gurus, I did not get the answers I was looking for.

Desperate, I began pouring my heart out to an attendee during a break. I told him that I had been getting chewed up lately. I explained that I could not catch a trend to save my life. The gentleman instantly replied, "Have you been plotting the S&P 500?" Everyday! I quipped back. He looked at me with a puzzled look and then said "And, you did not notice that it has gone sideways for the last three months? "

Right then it hit me. When you find yourself in a drawdown, making a lot of mistakes, and unable to make something happen, stop trading. Ask yourself is it me? Or, just the markets? It is amazing how clear your thinking will become when you stop taking a beating.

It Is You

If you have a loss, it is your fault not the market's. No invisible hand forced you to make a trade. It did not show up at your house and make you an offer that you could not refuse. You have to be accountable for you. You decide when to trade and when not to trade. And again, by not trading in less than ideal conditions, you take control of the situation when it is the market.

YOU WILL NEVER GET IT EXACTLY RIGHT — PERFECTIONISTS NEED NOT APPLY

If you are a perfectionist, it is going to be a lot tougher. You will never get it exactly right. You will never sell your long position at the exact top. You will never cover a short at the exact bottom. You have to learn to deal with the imperfect nature of trading. You have to be willing to be wrong. Operating in an uncertain environment is not easy. This is especially true for those coming from professions that require a high degree of accuracy. A surgeon would not last very long if he lost half of his patients. Yet in trading, you will often be wrong more than half of the time, but can still be successful.

FREEDOM IS NOT FREE

In trading, you and only you call the shots. You determine when to trade and when to sit on your hands. You determine how much to risk, where you will get in and when to get out. You answer only to yourself. It is the ultimate freedom. But freedom carries a price. Not having anyone to share the blame is very stressful. You are the king of your kingdom. Be warned though, heavy is the head that wears the crown.

BELIEVE IN WHAT YOU SEE AND NOT IN WHAT YOU BELIEVE

Successful people look for the good in things. They see what is right. This trait is detrimental to the success of a professional trader. People who possess it will look for reasons to support their position in spite of the market. Suppose you buy a stock and then it drops five days in a row. Then, it has an up day. You will breathe a sigh of relief, convincing yourself that the worst is over. This selective perception will kill you. What is, is. Executing a plan without putting your own personal beliefs into the market is not easy. However, your success will only come when you learn to believe in what you see and not in what you believe.

"It sounds very easy to say that all you have to do is to watch the tape, establish your resistance points and be ready to trade along the line of least resistance as soon as you have determined it. But in actual practice a man has to guard against many things, and most of all against himself — that is, against human nature."
- Reminiscences of a Stock Operator

"We have met the enemy and he is us."
- Pogo

"It is no surprise to me, I am my own worst enemy. 'Cause every now and then I kick the living sh*t out of me"
-Lit

MOST OF HELL IS SELF CREATED

In trading, you are your own worst enemy. Your job is to read the charts to understand the psychology of the masses, but at the same time resist acting on your own personal fear and greed. It is not an easy task.

If you are going through a string of losses, you will find yourself taking profits early on the next profitable position to avoid having it turn into yet another loss. You then watch in anguish as the stock takes off without you. You begin to think, if I would have just stayed with the position, it would have erased all the prior losses. So, you jump back in thinking you do not want to miss the train. Unfortunately, that turns out to be the exact top. You will then continue to make one bad decision after another as long as you let your emotions take charge.

Again, start small and build. If you are trading at a very small size it should be easy for you to execute your plan while resting your own personal fear and greed. And trust me, you will create a lot less hell for yourself.

YOU KNOW WHAT YOU ARE DOING WRONG

> *"A stock speculator sometimes makes mistakes and knows that he is making them."*
> -Reminiscences of A Stock Operator

Whenever I work with someone one on one, I wonder if I will be able to determine what this person is doing wrong. So, I ask. To my surprise, almost invariably, they tell me. And when they do not, I review their trades to see if I can find anything. Obvious things quickly jump out at me. I will see that they are taking trades against the trend, without sector confirmation, or in dull markets. They are overtrading or day trading. They are taking small profits rather than letting them ride. They are not honoring their stops. Their errors are blatant.

When I point out one or more of the above to them, they instantly say, "I know, I know." The solution then becomes very simple. Stop fighting the market, let the profits ride, and honor your stops. You do not need me to tell you this, because you know, you know!

BE CAREFUL TRADING AROUND MAJOR LIFE EVENTS

As I said in *Dave Landry On Swing Trading*, you must be careful when trading around major life events. It does not have to be something traumatic like the death of a loved one. It can be something positive like graduating from college or adopting a child. For me, it was the birth of my first daughter which ironically occurred a few minutes after the first time that the Nasdaq closed above 5,000 (and the next day was the last, so far!). I felt like Jack on the front of the Titanic. I was invincible. My trading became reckless. But wait, I thought you just said "You must be present to win?" Yes, you must be present to win but chances are, if you are under stress, you will not be in the proper state of mind to recognize these opportunities anyway. Avoiding trades around major life events, especially if you are a hot mess.

I was losing money hand over fist. I did not see the initial signs that the greatest bull market of the twentieth century was quickly coming to an end. I was busy as part of a team working to launch and grow an Internet site for traders, writing my first book, and advising hedge funds.

My new daughter was colicky and at night would only turn to me for comfort. I was getting by on very little sleep. In spite of all this, I continued to actively trade. Since I found myself doing the same things that I preach about not doing, I begin to scale back my trading. Soon, I was not trading at all. I had to stop the bleeding.

It was then that I had my greatest epiphany. Not being a participant, I found myself observing the markets very objectively. I saw stocks, sectors, and indices all setting up. Finally, I reached a point where I simply could not stand it anymore. I had to take action. I stepped in and was immediately rewarded with nice profits. I got too busy to actively manage the positions, so I let trailing stops take me out. To my surprise, I ended up staying with the positions longer than I normally would. I was able to ride out larger moves. I was simply too busy to outsmart the market and micromanage myself out of winning positions. I would continue to focus on all the tasks I was juggling until finally, I could not stand it anymore. All the pieces began to come together — sectors, indices, and individual stocks. I placed my trades and was once again immediately rewarded with profits. I began to repeat the above process over and over again. It felt like the trader in *Market Wizards* who said he simply "waited until there was money lying in the corner and then walked over and picked it up."

PSYCHOLOGICAL CHECKLIST
We are all prone to make emotional mistakes. Check the following before making your next trade. Do this until it becomes second nature. The next time you find yourself in a slump, re-read this, and return to the basics.

1. Are market conditions favorable for your methodology at the moment? For trend following, this means that the market has been trending and not trading sideways. Draw your arrows and apply the Rip Van Winkle "sleep test."

2. Are you following sound money management? Remember, money management will cure a multitude of sins. It will keep you in the game until the sun shines on you and your methodology.

3. Have you lived through a variety of market conditions? If you have only experienced a bull market, then trust me, you do not know what it is like to be in a bear. We are all human, it is impossible not to get excited when things are going well and depressed when things are not. Knowing that market conditions change can help temper these emotions.

4.   Do you know your methodology? Knowing that your methodology has the potential to stop you out numerous times before catching the mother of all trends makes it a lot easier to handle losses when they occur.

5.   Are you straying from your methodology? If you are trading my swing-to-intermediate method, then you should not be making numerous trades daily. You should not be buying markets because they are oversold or shorting them because they are overbought.

6.   Have you been trying to outsmart the market by getting in too early and exiting at the first minor signs of adversity? In other words, are you not following your plan?

7.   Do you even have a plan?

8.   Are you trading the best and leaving the rest?

9.   Are you dealing with any major or not so major life events?

10. You know what you are doing wrong. What is it?

CHAPTER 7

May I Have
Your Order Please?

BROKERAGES

Since we are looking for a longer term gain on every trade, any broker that can fill your order quickly and at a fair price is acceptable. I would suggest sticking with the major players. Your commissions might be a little higher, but as a general statement, you will get better fills and service. This will more than compensate for the added costs. Large brokerages also tend to have more shares to borrow for shorting stocks. Once you know what to expect from one of the big boys, you can experiment with smaller ones to see if they can provide you with similar services at a reduced rate. As a general rule, I would suggest keeping the majority of your money with a major brokerage.

Since I use mostly market and stop orders, I do not bother with direct access. For my methodology, direct access will often do more harm than good. I have worked with many traders who have missed great trades by trying to shave a few pennies off of their entry price. Keep in mind the old hedge fund adage "don't trip over the nickels while going for the dollars." I, like many traders, have discovered that some of the best trades come from the worst fills. It is a "be careful what you wish for" situation. If you get a good price, chances are the guy on the other side of the trade was looking to unload his stock for a reason. Conversely, if you have to pay up, it may be because someone is reluctant to let go of the inventory. Usually, when a stock is moving, it does not pause long for you to get on. Do not quibble over price.

EXECUTION OF ORDERS

You should use three types of orders: market orders, stop orders and, on occasion, limit orders.

MARKET ORDERS

During market hours, a market order will fill almost instantly. You are agreeing to the current ask for buying or the current bid for selling. If you are using discretion to enter or exit a stock, then use market orders. If you want in, you get in. If you need to get out, then get out.

STOP LOSS ORDERS

Once in a trade, you should always use protective stops. This way if something bad happens, the market will take you out of your position. A stop market order will become a market order when it triggers, and newer traders will generally find that having the order in the market will keep them from becoming the proverbial "deer in the headlights" during adverse market moves. The market will make the decision for you. You might not be happy that the market took you out, but at least you are not watching as losses continue to mount.

More advanced traders who prefer a little more discretion can use mental stops. The stop is not actually placed in the market but the trader will exit the position at the market if the market trades around where an actual stop would have be placed. An alarm can be set near the stop to alert you that the position may need to be exited. Mental stops are often used when looking to give a stock a little more or less wiggle room. We will explore discretionary techniques later.

Although stops are usually associated with exiting positions, they can also be quite useful for entries. Referring to Figure 7.1, suppose you watch a stock open (a) and it does not immediately trigger. You can place a stop market order at your entry (b). This order will become a market order if hit. You can then go about your business and the market will trigger a position should the stock trade at or above the entry. This will help you to avoid missing a trade and keep you from watching a screen all day. And, once again, you let the market make the decision for you.

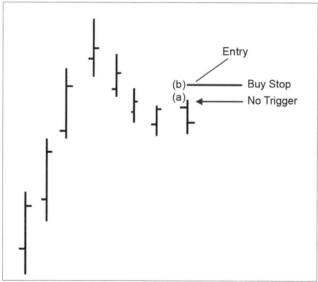

Figure 7.1 ~ Entry Using A Stop

Limit Orders
A limit order will get you in or out of a stock at a certain price or better. Although this sounds great, you should rarely use them. In fact, the only time I think you should consider using a limit order is when you are looking to take partial profits. You can place a limit at your initial profit target. This is illustrated in Figure 7.2. On occasion, you will get lucky and this order can fill on a spike type move. This is especially true in choppy markets when noise alone tags your initial profit target.

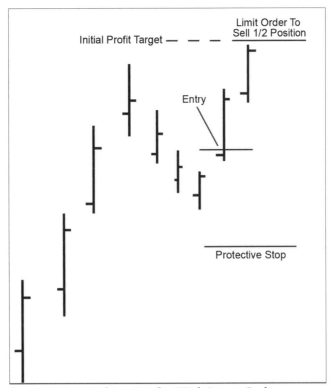

Figure 7.2 ~ Taking Profits With Limit Orders

Using a limit order to enter trades can be a recipe for disaster. In fast market conditions, your trigger price may only be available for a moment. If you are not the very first order in line, and someone else gets filled for all the available shares at your limit price, then there will be no shares for you as the market moves away. During momentum markets, this can cause you to miss the best trades and get tagged into the worst. The good ones zoom past your entry and leave you behind, while the bad ones hit the trigger price and reverse to fill you into a stock that winds up moving toward your stop rather than your target.

I also never use a protective stop limit order. This order will fill you if the stop is hit, but only if the limit price is still available. For protective stops, this can keep you in a market during a fast adverse move. If the stop limit is hit and there are no shares available at your limit price, the order will not get executed. You will be stuck with a position that you should have exited. Using a stop limit for entries is also a bad idea. Some of my biggest winners have come from some of my worst fills. Demand (or supply for shorts) is so great that the stock triggers and never looks back. Unless your stop limit to enter is very liberal (e.g. the limit price is well above the stop for longs), a great trade can be missed in the blink of an eye.

CARRYING ORDERS OVERNIGHT

I recommend that you do not carry orders overnight. Opening gap reversals can often occur and needlessly trigger a bad trade. If your have an exit stop in place before the market opens, it could get triggered on a bad tick (i.e. an erroneous or suspect trade), fast move, or an opening gap reversal and cause your open position to be closed out. I recommend waiting for a stock to open and then entering your protective stop, entry stops, and limits for profit targets (if used).

Think Before You Click

Remember that a stop order to buy (or cover a short) must be placed above the market otherwise it will instantly become a market order. Conversely, a stop order to sell (or sell short) must be placed below the market, or it will instantly become a market order. Limit orders can be even more dangerous. A limit order to sell a stock must be placed above the market. A limit order to buy a stock must be placed below where the stock is trading. If not, market makers will quickly snap it up, gladly taking advantage of your mistake. For instance, suppose a stock is trading at $50 and you put in a limit order to buy at $55. This means that you want the stock at $55 or below. Your order says that you are willing to pay $5 more than the stock is currently worth. A market maker can quickly snap that up, selling you the stock at $55 to fill your order. He profits and you are now faced with an instant $5 per share loss.

Some brokerages have checks and balances to keep you from making mistakes on your orders. I would advise that you do not count on them. Think before you click.

Summary

Stop and market orders can be used to efficiently enter and exit trades. Limit orders should be used sparingly, and only for taking partial profits. Again, remember to think before you click so you do not end up with a trade that you do not want, or worst give up your hard earned money by offering to buy at a premium or sell at a bargain above or below the prices warranted by the market.

Plan Your Trade

It is critical that you plan your trade and trade your plan. You cannot wing it. You must know where you will get in, where you will take partial profits, and what type of discretionary techniques you will use. The more planning you put into a trade, the less likely you are to make mistakes or micromanage yourself out of a big winner.

Planning your trades also gives you a great reference. If you work hard, I promise you that you will get better and better over time. Like me, you will look back at trades and think, "what the heck was I thinking?" Careful planning makes reviewing positions very easy. Traders who plan their work can look back over years of trading in a snap and make adjustments when the market and the strategy get out of step.

I have outlined the things you should consider about the stock and the sector before entering a trade. Fill out this sheet on each and every trade.

PLAN THE TRADE

Stock_____ Buy__ Sell Short __ Pattern _____ Entry _____

Protective Stop _____ Initial Profit Target_____ Trailing Stop (how) _____

Confirmation of Trend (or Transition) from Market_____Sector_____Other stocks within sector_____

How are you? Are there any major (or not so major!) crises in your life?

Notes:

Gray Area
Describe what discretionary techniques you might consider (e.g. Front running, OGRe entries, etc... see Taking The Next Steps). Keep in mind that the larger the "gray area" the more decisions you will be faced with during the heat of battle. Items that re-occur frequently here should become part of the "Plan Your Trade" section.

TRADE THE PLAN

Actual: Entry _____ Initial Protective Stop_____

Where did you take partial profits (if offered)_____

Did you honor your stop?_____

How/Where did you trail your stop? _____

Notes:

POST MORTEM

Did you deviate from the plan?

Was this deviation profitable?

Was it following sound trading practices?

How are you?

Notes:

Section I
Closing Thoughts

The original goal of this book was to help the layman avoid the common pitfalls of following conventional wisdom and to protect him from urges of human nature itself. I feel confident that you now have those tools. Even if you have no intention of becoming a trader, you now know how to think like one. You will not be persuaded by analysts or the media. You now know that the markets do not always go up longer term. You know how to look at charts to see if a market is trending. You know that markets are made up of emotional participants — just like you. You know that logic often does not apply. You know that anyone could be wrong about what the market will do next. You know not to impose your own will onto the market. You know that you must have a plan and more importantly, you must follow it.

GETTING BACK TO THE LAYMAN

So why did the layman buy Apple? He bought an iPhone and loved it. Everyone he knew loved it too. He saw iPhones everywhere he went. He figured that Apple must be selling a ton of them. He was right. They were. Shortly after the layman bought Apple, they announced the best earnings in the history of the company. Unfortunately, the stock which has been sliding, continued its decline.

If, like the layman, you like your iPhone and think that Apple might be a good company to buy, you need to first pull up the chart to make sure that the market agrees with you. A stock must be trending and set up before you buy it. The broader market and the stock's sector must also headed higher for the trade to make sense. You need to wait for the stock to prove itself by resuming its trend and triggering an entry. If your timing is wrong, your protective stops should take care of you. And if you are right, then partial profits will gratify you when they are available, and you will have no problem riding out a long-term winner using trailing stops.

A BETTER APPROACH

If you really want to capture big trends in stocks, you cannot watch just a few issues and wait around for them to trend. You might be waiting a long time or even forever. Successful traders utilize the entire universe of thousands of stocks and let the right setups in the right issues determine the plan.

Let the opportunity come to you. Charts do not lie. As the next big thing catches on, the stock of the new star will trend higher as more and more people jump on board. Opportunity will not always be as obvious as the iPhone. It might be a maker of yoga clothes instead. Logic will not always apply either. When the whole world is running out of energy and oil will soon be $200 barrel, you might find that the best opportunities lie in shorting the energy stocks.

TAKING THE NEXT STEP

Even if you have no intention of becoming a trader, I would urge you to take the next step and study the following more advanced concepts. Knowing them will help you make even better decisions. Instead of waiting around to buy another Apple, you can scan to find the next great stock, already ripe for the picking. You can use advanced transitional patterns to get on these trends early. Once these treasures are found, you can apply discretionary techniques to help you avoid false moves, stay with winners, and to help mitigate damages on the occasional large losing trade.

SECTION II
Taking The Next Step

CHAPTER 8
Treasure Hunting: Finding The Next Big Trend

With thousands of publicly traded stocks, trying to pick the few that have potential can be overwhelming. The good news is that you can quickly eliminate more than 80 percent of the candidates by simply requiring adequate volume, price, and volatility. The remaining 20 percent are culled further by requiring the stock to be set up, have great trending characteristics, and sector confirmation. These stringent criteria will eliminate the vast majority of issues. In fact, in less-than-ideal conditions, there will likely be very few or even no worthy candidates remaining. Let's break it down.

VOLUME

I have yet to find a use for volume as a predictive tool. For the sake of brevity, I am not going to go into a thesis as to why. To those interested in studying volume, I would encourage them to study the works of writers whose research goes against conventional wisdom, such as Richard Arms. Be warned though, even if you find a use for volume, other factors such as competing exchanges, derivatives, algorithmic trading and so-called dark pools make it difficult if not impossible to know exactly what the true volume is. I only use volume to determine if the stock is liquid enough to trade.

Smaller capitalization stocks have the potential to make large moves because there is only so much stock to go around. Unfortunately, if the volume is too small, you face a liquidity problem. It is possible that there will not be anyone on the other side of your trade unless you are willing to pay more or sell at bargain. In other words, the difference between the bid price and the ask price, the spread, can be quite large.

Large capitalization stocks do not have liquidity problems because there are plenty of participants buying and selling. However, they tend to cancel out each other. This makes it difficult for the stock to have persistent trends and trade cleanly. In other words, the more players in a market, the more the stock tends to chop around.

As a general rule, I like to see stocks with a 50-day average volume of at least 500,000 shares. This provides enough liquidity for buying, selling, and shorting. I will occasionally dip below this number if I really like the setup, especially for buys. In trading, there is always a trade off.

Thinner issues can provide great opportunities as they are discovered. However, the spreads will likely be much worse than those of issues with higher volume. Further, lower volume stocks could be prone to manipulation or could make large adverse moves when a large trader wants out and there is no one there willing to take the other side of the trade. Considering this, experienced aggressive traders might occasionally consider smaller cap issues. However, I would encourage them to keep volume to a minimum of at least 100,000 shares on average. Anything less and you will likely face more and more problems associated with low liquidity.

I also *prefer* stocks that trade less than 2 million shares per day. I do not use an upper limit on volume, as very large cap issues can trend nicely. I find this is an exception, but it is still worth studying the charts of the big volume movers.

PRICE

Short term traders tend to focus more on dollar moves than percent moves. They are in and out, looking to capture fractional gains quickly. They tend to trade higher priced stocks, which have the ability to move around more, and tend to trade more cleanly. In my first book, I stated that I only like to trade stocks that are "$20 and preferably $30 or higher." Since then, my trading time frame has become progressively longer. In recent years, I stopped focussing exclusively on high priced stocks. The lingering bear market in 2007 - 2009 left very few high priced stocks to trade anyway, and even in 2010, lower prices are the norm. Now I focus on stocks with a price of at least $3. This is low enough to catch emerging opportunities, but high enough to weed out the extremely speculative so called Penny Stocks.

VOLATILITY

Volatility is simply how much a stock moves around over a given period. My favorite way to measure this is with historical volatility — also known as statistical volatility. This provides a standardized measurement. It allows me to compare apples to apples when looking at different stocks. Historical volatility (HV) is available in most charting packages.

Since we are looking to capture both short and longer term moves, stocks with higher volatility readings can provide better opportunities. However, there can be too much of a good thing. Stocks with extreme HV readings are dangerous and should be avoided. I usually exercise extreme caution when the HV is over 100.

Keep in mind that volatility is relative. Ten years ago I liked stocks with a 50-day HV reading of at least 40 or higher. When the volatility of the market dried up I found myself trading stocks with HV readings in the 20's and 30's. Volatility has since come back and I am once again focusing mostly on HV levels of 40 and higher.

The overall market is a good gauge of where you should be looking for opportunities based on volatility. The HV of the stocks you trade should be higher than the broader market. In Wall Street lingo, stocks that meet this criteria are said to have a high beta.

TRENDING CHARACTERISTICS

In addition to being set up, any stock you consider should be in a strong trend or at least making an obvious transition in trend. It should have many Trend Qualifiers with the trend and few against it. The stock should trade cleanly. When it trends, it should exhibit persistency. It should make strong directional moves, pullback, and then trend again. Price should not bounce wildly. If the chart looks like an electrocardiogram, then it is not a stock that trades cleanly.

Stock personalities can and do change, but you should focus your attention on symbols that have demonstrated a clear propensity to trend and trade smoothly in the past. When trying to decide between two setups you feel are equally attractive, study the past performance of each stock and pick the one that had the cleanest charts in the past. If you still can not decide and like both setups equally, pick the one with the highest HV.

CONFIRMATION IN RELATED STOCKS AND SECTOR CONFIRMATION

The sector action should confirm the action that you're seeing in an individual stock. It too should be trending and ideally set up. Further, since a sector index can occasionally be moved by just a few select issues, you want to make sure that other stocks within that sector are also trending. The more confirmation within the sector and similar stocks, the better. Just as a rising tide lifts all boats for the overall market, the same holds true for the sector. In fact, sector confirmation is even more important. There is one caveat. Early leaders can emerge within a sector, forming trend transitional patterns long before the sector begins to trend. Ideally though, even with transitional patterns, you should have some confirmation from the sector and other stocks within the sector.

NIGHTLY ANALYSIS

I like looking at charts — lots of charts. This gives me a feel for what is going on in stocks, sectors, and the overall market. Many times, things that might not be so obvious in the overall market or sectors, will really pop out when flipping through hundreds of charts. You might start seeing stocks in selected groups begin to break down long before the sector or the overall market begins to turn. For example, in fall of 2007, I began to see mostly short trades setting up in spite of a market near all-time highs. In spring of 2008, I saw oils stocks set up as shorts even though the underlying commodity continued to rocket higher. In the spring of 2009, I began seeing a lot of longs setting up in a variety of areas in spite of the market remaining in a longer term downtrend

Except for the occasional moving average, I don't use any indicators. I keep it simple. More often than not, my charts are blank (i.e. no indicators). Therefore, although I use and recommend a specific charting package, you should be able to accomplish your analysis with almost any charting package. You get what you pay for, but for those just getting started, there are even free charting packages available on the Internet.

TOP DOWN IN A BOTTOM UP FASHION

Top down analysis is just that. You start at the top with the overall market and then work your way down through sectors and to individual stocks. First, you make sure the market is trending. Then, you study the sectors to see which ones are trending. And finally, you look for individual stocks within those sectors for opportunities. Ideally, the market, sector and stock should all be headed in the same direction.

My approach to top down analysis is slightly unorthodox. It is actually bottom up. Instead of starting at the top and working my way down, I do the opposite. I start by looking at a large number of individual stocks, I then look at hundreds of sectors, and finally I study the major indices. This gives me an edge over those who only look at a few select areas. I know what is really going on under the hood. This allows me to see old trends ending and new ones emerging long before most individual traders. I believe that by doing the same, you can become a better trader.

CREATING MY TRADABLE UNIVERSE

I run a very basic scan that identifies stocks above a certain price (currently set to $3 per share) and with a minimum 50-day average volume (currently set to 500,000 shares). This creates a tradable universe. The results of this scan can vary but it usually results in 1500-2000 stocks. This eliminates nearly 80 percent of all symbols in my database. This scan only has to be run once a week.

I sort this list by 50-day historical volatility. This shows me the most volatile stocks first. This causes the cream to rise to the top. I like to flip though these at least once daily. Although this might seem like a lot of stocks, it really only takes about 20 to 30 minutes to go through all of them. Keep in mind that I am not doing in depth analysis on each and every chart. I am quickly flipping through them to see if there is anything that might look remotely interesting. Also, those stocks toward the bottom of the list are less interesting to me because their volatility is lower. The further I get into the list, the more I tend to pick up my pace, knowing that I want to be focused on those issues that have the tendency to be more volatile than the overall market. Again, I am not doing much in-depth analysis here. I am simply looking for something that is set up or something that could setup up soon — either trending or forming an obvious transition.

When I spot candidates, I flag the interesting ones and then copy them to a separate watch list which I call my Landry 100. Once the list gets over 100 stocks, I prune it back, removing stocks that are no longer trending. This gives me a relatively small manageable list to monitor.

RUN A PULLBACK SCAN

After the close, I run a simple pullback scan on my tradeable universe. This scan looks for recent (not today) 20-day highs or recent 20-day lows. This will catch virtually all of my patterns. It can produce 500 to 1,000 stocks or more. I sort these by historical volatility. Like my tradable universe, I go through this list quickly, flagging anything interesting. Once the volatility drops below the overall market, I pick up the pace even further, knowing that I have likely already seen the stocks that have the best opportunities. I copy anything flagged to my Landry 100 watch list.

ANALYZE IPOS

We discussed earlier that initial public offerings (IPO's), with their limited bad memories, can provide great opportunities. I love them. Unfortunately, there are not enough of them to make IPO's my primary focus. During poor market conditions, companies usually hold off on going public, further restricting the opportunities.

I look at all new IPOs that have come public over the last 50 days. Fifty is arbitrary, but I use it as a cutoff as my main scans require 50-days of data. After 50 days, these stocks will be picked up by my software. I copy any that have been met with enthusiasm and are trending higher to my Top 100.

ANALYZE LANDRY 100

I move on to analyze my Landry 100. I slow my pace down a bit and look at each and every stock a little more carefully. I pay attention to the trend or transition and look to see if it has recently been trading smoothly. I back the chart out to see if it has traded cleanly in the past. I overlay the sub-sector on the chart and look for confirmation of a broader trend or the presence of a transition. If a stock looks like it has potential, I make a note of it. In the margins of my notebook, I write the sector next to the stock symbol. I usually make at least one more pass through my Landry 100, making sure I did not miss anything. Then I take my list from my notebook to create a watch list for the next trading day. I dub this my Landry List.

Before I shift my analysis to the Landry List, I note where stocks are stacking up. For instance, on April 2, 2009 my list was as follows:

Banks:	SBIB
Metals & Mining:	FCX
Retail:	DDS,TJX
Insurance:	XL
Energy:	ATPG,BRY,DRQ,OII,PCZ
Hardware:	STX
Durables:	ETH
Non-Durables:	PVH
Leisure:	LTM
Financial:	CME

Notice that more stocks in the energy sector are set up than in other groups. From a quick glance at my notebook, I know that I want to focus my attention here for the next trading day. I research this sector by studying its components. If the sector is very large, I might sort the stocks by price and volume to weed out what is thinly traded or cheap. On a smaller sector, I look at all stocks that make it up. I am looking to see if other stocks confirm what I perceive to be happening. I am also looking to see if there is anything similar in the group that I might have overlooked. Anything that looks interesting is flagged and copied to my Landry 100. If it is genuinely intriguing, I add it directly to my Landry List.

By observing where most potential opportunities are stacking up, I get a head start on my sector analysis. If I have ten energy stocks and only one retail, I probably will concentrate on stocks in the energies. By looking at so many stocks, I back into my sector analysis and have a good idea what I should focus on.

SECTOR ANALYSIS

Just like I enjoy looking at a lot of stocks, I like to look at all the sectors every day. I use Morningstar Industry Groups available in Telechart. These are sector indices made up of stocks within the individual groups. There are 249 of these sector indices ranging from Accident and Health Insurance to Wireless Communications. I flag those that are trending, setting up, breaking out or breaking down. I note those sectors that are simply trading sideways.

SECTOR RELATIVE STRENGTH ANALYSIS

Relative strength (RS) represents just what the name implies. It shows the strength of one market versus another. For instance, suppose the benchmark S&P 500 is up 5 percent over a given period. Sectors that are up more than 5 percent over that same period are outperforming the overall market and have a high relative strength. Conversely, sectors which are up less than 5 percent have been under performing the overall market and exhibit low RS.

At least once per week, I sort my database by RS of the Morningstar Industry Groups versus the S&P 500. I look at a variety of time frames. I pick a significant low or high in the S&P and study that period forward. For instance, the S&P 500 made a multi-year low in November of 2008. In Figure 8.1, this is the starting point (a). Measuring to the current trading day (b), we see that the market gained 4.39 percent during the period (from 11/21/09 to 02/12/09). Essentially, the market has gone sideways. However, looking to our sector performance, we see that Semiconductor-Memory has gained over 97 percent during this time (c). Going down this list, we see that Silver has gained over 80 percent and Gold has gained over 50 percent.

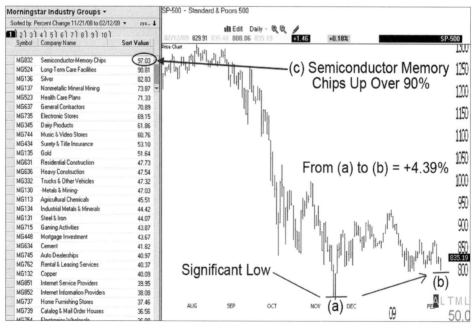

Figure 8.1   *Chart Created With Telechart Platinum*

Now, let's scroll down to the bottom of the sector list. We see that while the market was up 4.39 percent, the Regional Banks-Mid Atlantic lost over 32 percent of their value. Most of the stocks near the bottom of this list are bank related (Figure 8.2).

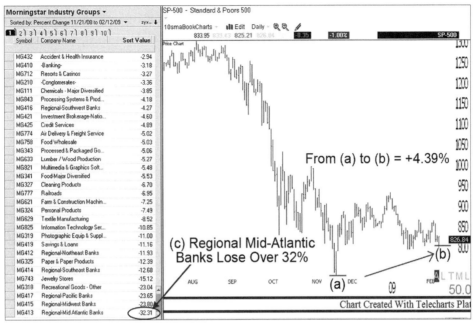

Figure 8.2   *Chart Created With Telechart Platinum*

From this instant scan we know that Semiconductors-Memory, Long-term Care Facilities, Silver, Nonmetallic Mining, and Healthcare Plans are doing exceptionally well and Regional Banks, Recreational Goods, and Jewelry Stores are under performing.

Relative strength sorts are a great way to find strength and weakness in the sectors. However, keep in mind that strength or weakness based on RS does not imply that the behavior will continue. Weak stocks can strengthen and strong stocks can weaken. Therefore, change or "delta" in RS is also important.

Before we discuss delta RS, let's look at an example in weather. Suppose I tell you that it is 32 degrees outside. If you are from the south like me, you will probably instantly think that is cold. However, if I told you that 30 minutes ago, it was 20 degrees, you then have a new piece of information. Yes, it is still cold, but it is getting warmer.

Just like the temperature, stocks heat up and cool off. Therefore, it is a good idea to run RS scans for both the short and longer term. This will show you what is hot and what is not as well as where things are heating up or cooling down.

Referring to Figure 8.3, from the March low on 03/06/09 to 05/19/09, the S&P gained 32.89 percent (a to b). Over the same period, Resorts and Casinos have gained over 211 percent (c).

Figure 8.3   *Chart Created With Telechart Platinum*

However, in Figure 8.4 we see that the last few weeks of trading from (a) 05/05/09 to (b) 05/19/09 we see that the S&P has gained .48 percent, but Resorts and Casinos, the best performer longer term, was actually the worst performer shorter-term, losing 16 percent (c).

Resorts & Casinos, which have outperformed the market longer-term by gaining over 200 percent in several months (Figure 8.3), were actually the worst performing sector shorter-term, losing 16 percent of their value over the last few weeks (Figure 8.4). This is why it is important to look over a variety of periods.

Although I still like to look at each and every sector chart, the RS sorts often help to point out sectors that I might have overlooked. On occasion, there might be hidden strength or weakness. This is particularly true in choppy markets.

ANALYZING EXCHANGE TRADED FUNDS

There are nearly 800 Exchange Traded Funds with new ones being added almost daily. Since many are not tradable because they have low volume, I sort them by their 5-day volume. I use this narrow window because I will be alerted to any new liquid ETF's soon after they come onto the market. Keep in mind that I am not using volume as a predictive tool. I am only using it weed out the less meaningful securities. I proceed to flip through the first 150 or so ETF's. The ETF sectors might paint a different picture than other sector indices.

The great thing about ETF's is that they are not limited to groups of stocks representing sectors or indices. They also exist for bonds, commodities, foreign indices, and currencies. When stocks begin to behave erratically, setups in these ETF's may be worthy of consideration as alternative investments. Since most people are long oriented (i.e. they do not short), some of

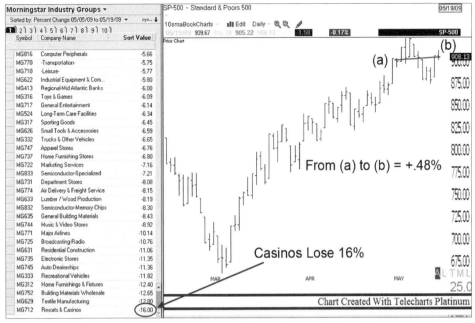

Symbol	Company Name	Sort Value
MG816	Computer Peripherals	-5.66
MG770	-Transportation-	-5.75
MG710	-Leisure-	-5.77
MG622	Industrial Equipment & Com...	-5.80
MG413	Regional-Mid Atlantic Banks	-6.00
MG316	Toys & Games	-6.09
MG717	General Entertainment	-6.14
MG524	Long-Term Care Facilities	-6.34
MG317	Sporting Goods	-6.45
MG626	Small Tools & Accessories	-6.59
MG332	Trucks & Other Vehicles	-6.65
MG747	Apparel Stores	-6.76
MG737	Home Furnishing Stores	-6.80
MG722	Marketing Services	-7.16
MG833	Semiconductor-Specialized	-7.21
MG731	Department Stores	-8.08
MG774	Air Delivery & Freight Service	-8.15
MG633	Lumber / Wood Production	-8.19
MG832	Semiconductor-Memory Chips	-8.30
MG635	General Building Materials	-8.43
MG744	Music & Video Stores	-8.92
MG771	Major Airlines	-10.14
MG725	Broadcasting-Radio	-10.76
MG631	Residential Construction	-11.06
MG735	Electronic Stores	-11.35
MG745	Auto Dealerships	-11.36
MG333	Recreational Vehicles	-11.82
MG312	Home Furnishings & Fixtures	-12.40
MG752	Building Materials Wholesale	-12.65
MG629	Textile Manufacturing	-12.80
MG712	Resorts & Casinos	-16.00

Figure 8.4   *Chart Created With Telechart Platinum*

the creators of ETF's have issued inverse securities. They go up when the index they represent goes down and vise versa. This allows you to effectively go short an index through buying. The fact that the chart trades contra to the index can give you a different perspective. For instance, if an inverse index ETF looks bullish, then the index outlook is actually bearish. This can be very helpful, especially when you have a strong bias.

Many of the ETF's are stock index related. By looking at them every day, I back into my index analysis. I have a good feel for the Dow through the Diamonds (DIA), the S&P through the (SPY) and the Nasdaq 100 through the "Q's" (QQQQ). This also allows me to see broader based indices such as the Russell 2000 (IWM), which I would not normally analyze in my work.

KEEPING MARKET ANALYSIS SIMPLE

In the early 1990's, I spent many years researching mechanical systems, especially for market timing. I Figured since I had a degree in computer science, I might as well use it. I assumed that there had to be a way to mechanize trading. And, if I looked hard enough, I would find the holy grail. Since there are those who will only believe something if it is quantified, I was encouraged to put some of my mechanical systems research into my first book.

Since then, I have been a 100 percent discretionary trader. I no longer try to mechanize things. I have learned that there is no holy grail and common sense is your best friend. I found that mechanical systems are great within a certain context of the market. However, conditions change and so must the trader. As an example, I have systems that I built based on the Volatility Index (VIX). It used to be a great predictor of stock prices and then it just seemed to stop working for a few years. I later discovered that this could be attributed to a large degree of leveraged funds using spreads. This means that they were buying one market and simultaneously selling another as soon as these markets began to move. This greatly compressed the volatility of the market. Their action could be equated to walking a dog on a leash. When it gets to one side of the sidewalk, a tug brings it back to the middle. I do not run the systems any more, but I do occasionally look at the VIX and I would venture to say that the VIX systems are once again working as volatility has increased. This increase could have been caused by a de-leveraging of the aforementioned spreaders. Metaphorically, the leash broke.

I am not taking a shot at those who develop and use mechanical systems. It is just that after many years of research, I have come to the realization that it is not for me. I think markets change and traders need to adapt. We can use our heads to make much better decisions than a computer. If the opposite were true, a company like IBM or Cray would own the market.

As you can see, my market analysis is really pretty simple. By the time I get to the big picture, I have already looked at thousands of stocks, hundreds of sectors, and numerous ETF's. Looking under the hood gives me a good feel for what the market should do. I then look at the major indices for the same things I look for in individual stocks. I seek to identify if they are trending, forming obvious transitions, or just chopping around. I look for support, resistance, and whether there are any technical patterns. I carefully look for any of my own patterns that may be setting up. Most importantly, I draw my arrows on the charts.

BIGGER PICTURE ANALYSIS MEANS SEEING THE FOREST

Several times a week, I look at the weekly and monthly index charts to make sure that the forest and the trees are still in plain sight. This helps maintain perspective and keeps me on the right side of the market. I look for the same factors that I looked for in the daily time frame.

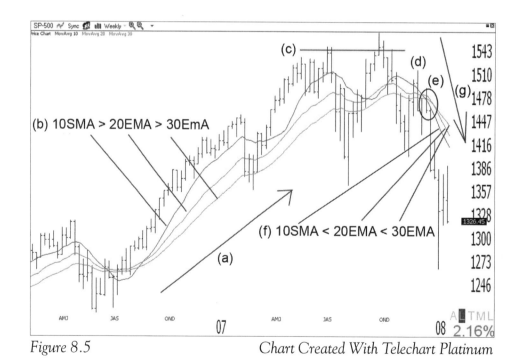

Figure 8.5   *Chart Created With Telechart Platinum*

Notice on the weekly S&P chart (Figure 8.5) that the market was in an uptrend from late-2006 to mid-2007. The arrow points up (a). Further, during this time, notice the Bowtie moving averages (see chapter 9) are in proper uptrend order-the 10SMA > 20 EMA >30 EMA. Then, notice the market sell-off, rally to marginal new highs, and then stall. This action creates a Double Top (c). The market sells off hard and then retraces back up, but stalls out (d) without reaching its prior highs. This action forms a more advanced pattern known as a Gatekeeper (see *Dave Landry's 10 Best Swing Trading Patterns & Strategies*). It then forms a Bowtie down (e). At this juncture, the moving averages have switched to downtrend proper order (f). And, most importantly, the big arrow has turned down (g).

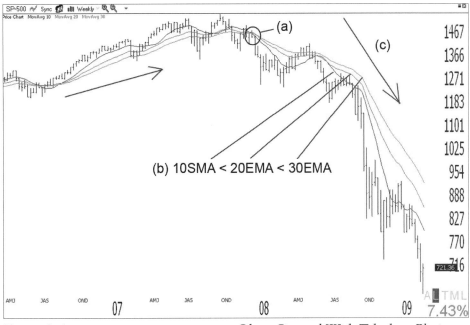

Figure 8.6   *Chart Created With Telechart Platinum*

Fast forwarding to March 2009 (figure 8.6), we see that one of the greatest bear markets in history began with a weekly Bowtie down in late-2007 (a). The Bowtie moving averages, with the exception of a slight kiss between the 10SMA and the 20EMA, have remained in downtrend proper order (b) since then. And of course, the big arrow (c) has pointed down.

Keep in mind that there is the potential for long lag times when using weekly and monthly charts. The daily will obviously turn long before the weekly and the monthly catch up. Therefore, you should trade from the daily chart but use longer-term charts to gain perspective.

One final point, although my market analysis is essentially the same as my individual stock analysis, trading the indices is often choppy when compared to individual stocks. They are an average of the representative stocks and the playing field contains many trading derivative issues (e.g. index futures, index options, exchange traded index funds). Therefore, you have to be a little more lenient with the technical patterns.

SUMMARY

With thousands of stocks to choose from, finding the next big winner can be daunting. The good news is the majority of stocks can be quickly eliminated by simply requiring adequate volume, price, and volatility. The remainder of these stocks can be reduced to a manageable list by requiring the stocks to be trending, set up, and have sector confirmation.

I use a top down approach applied in a bottom up manner. Beginning with individual stocks, I work my way into sectors, ETF's, and eventually the major market indices. By working my way up through all these charts, I get a good feel for what the stocks, the sectors, and the overall market will likely do next. I then look at longer-term index charts to gain perspective.

Although it might seem like a lot of work, for me it is like being on a treasure hunt. With a little practice and experience, it gets easier. You will soon find that the best setups will jump out at you. In fact, eventually you will know within a blink of the eye if a stock should be considered or tossed out.

CHAPTER 9

Getting Into New Trends Early: Trading Trend Transitions

When you catch a new trend early, the payoff can be huge. Unfortunately, since you are fighting what could turn out to be only be a correction in a longer-term trend, you have to realize that there will be a higher failure rate than trading pullbacks in established trends. Therefore, I would encourage you to get good at trading pullbacks in established trends before looking to trade transitions in trend. Like the pioneers, when trading transitions you are either going to get the gold or the arrows. I think the chance for gold makes it all worthwhile.

In addition to their higher failure rate, recognizing and trading transitions can be tough. I get more questions on my trend transition patterns than all of my others combined. Although I believe the following patterns will help you immeasurably, you will still need a little experience before you get it right consistently.

In *Dave Landry's 10 Best Swing Trading Strategies & Patterns* I said "Trends do not last forever. Eventually they exhaust themselves and quite often, a new trend in the opposite direction emerges. However, established trends can often last much longer and go much further than most anticipate. Trying to buy a stock because it is low or sell short a stock because it is high is a loser's game. The good news is that the stock will leave clues that a trend is turning and will usually have a minor correction before resuming its new trend. Looking to enter after that minor correction and only if the new trend shows signs of resuming is the goal of my transitional patterns." This is illustrated in Figure 9.1.

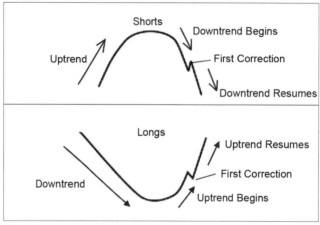

Figure 9.1

The extended bull markets of the late 1980's and 1990's spoiled the trend traders. Unfortunately, trends have not lasted as long since then. It is important to get aboard a new trend as soon as possible. It is also vitally important to recognize when an established trend may be coming to end. Although I have always been a fan of pullbacks in longer-term trends, my work over the last 10 years has focused more and more on catching these trend transitions. The following patterns will allow you to do just that.

FIRST THRUSTS

Markets in major trend transitions often begin with a sharp thrust in the new direction. This tends to catch participants off guard. Trapped on the wrong side of the market, they find themselves waiting for the market to reverse so they can get off the hook. Bottom pickers and top pickers who missed the top or bottom and do not want to pay up are also waiting for some sort of meaningful correction. Unfortunately for these traders, the meaningful correction may never come. Often, markets making a sharp thrust in a new direction only pull back very briefly before resuming their new trend. The old market participants will soon be forced out at adverse prices and the bottom/top pickers must pay up or risk being left behind. By waiting for the market to have a sharp thrust in the new direction, you avoid the pitfalls associated with picking tops/bottoms. By looking to enter at the first signs of a correction rather than waiting for something more substantial, there is the potential for your position to be helped along by the predicament of the aforementioned traders.

The goal of the First Thrust is to get on a new trend early. You wait for the market to make a strong thrust opposite the direction of its longer-term trend and then enter on the slightest correction. Entering new trends is risky, but the payoff can be tremendous when you catch a new trend early.

Here are the rules for buys. Short sales are reversed (Figure 9.2).

1. The stock must make a major new low. The more significant the low the better. Multi-year lows or ideally all-time lows (or highs for shorts) are my favorite. This helps to ensure the maximum numbers of traders are on the wrong side of the market when the trend begins to change (rule 2).

2. The stock must then rally sharply.

3. The stock needs to make a lower high and a lower low. The first sign of a correction is a one-bar pullback. If wide range bars higher dominated the first thrust it may only make a lower high. This can make for riskier trades since the stock has had very little correction. However, in trading, risk often comes with reward. These brief corrections give players very little time to get in. Most are waiting for a more meaningful pullback. Should the thrust resume after this brief pause, these traders must either jump in or risk being left behind.

4. Go long above the high of (3).

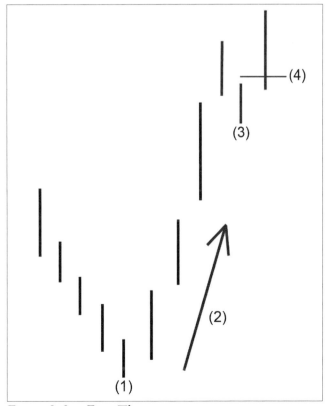

Figure 9.2 ~ First Thrust

Let's look at some examples.

Figure 9.3 ~ ELON   *Chart Created With Telechart Platinum*

1. In Figure 9.3, after drifting lower for years, energy product manufacturer Echelon Corp. (ELON) makes a multi-year low.

2. The stock has a sharp thrust from the bottom of its multi-year trading range. This corresponds precisely with 2007 bottom in crude oil.

3. The stock pulls back.

4. Enter as the trend resumes.

5. Although it is a bit of a wild ride, the stock doubles over the next few months and later triples in value.

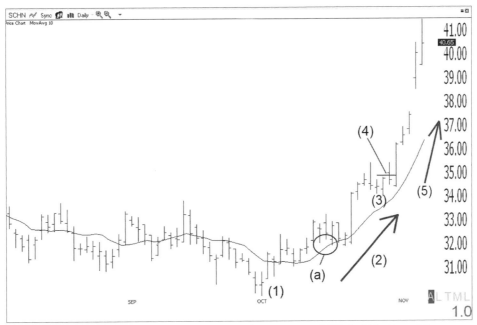

Figure 9.4 ~ SCHN   *Chart Created With Telechart Platinum*

1. In Figure 9.4, Schnitzer Steel (SCHN) hits 8-month lows.

2. After a slow start, the stock rallies sharply. There is a First Kiss After Daylight set up around this time (a). I will discuss the specifics of the First Kiss pattern later in this chapter.

3. The stock makes a lower low and a lower high — a one-day pullback.

4. Enter as the trend resumes.

5. The stock gains nearly 20 percent over the next few days. Following up: The stock then begins to trade sideways and later implodes (not shown). However, using proper money and position management this still would have made for a good trade.

The homebuilders set up as a First Thrust long before the media announced that the real estate bubble had burst.

Figure 9.5 ~ BZH   *Chart Created With Telechart Platinum*

1. In Figure 9.5, Beazer Homes USA (BZH) hits an all-time high.

2. The stock has a sharp selloff over the next few days.

3. The stock makes a higher high and a higher low. In other words, a one-day pullback.

4. Enter as the trend resumes.

5. BZH pulls back one more time and sets up a First Kiss After Daylight (discussed next).

6. The stock loses over 16 percent of its value over the next few weeks. In fact, this turns out to be a major top. It goes on to trade as low as 25 cents a share.

SUMMARY
New trends often begin with a bang. When this occurs, the stock may only pause briefly before taking off. While others are waiting for a more meaningful correction, nimble traders can take advantage of this by entering the new trend early. Although getting in a trend early is risky, the rewards can be enormous. There is a chance you will catch the next great bull market or be short as a bubble bursts.

PATTERN APPLICATION
This pattern works well on both the long and short sides of the market. However, since they slide faster than they glide, I tend to like the short side even more.

Ideally, the market and sector should also be making a sharp transition in trend. Occasionally though, early leaders can emerge long before the market and sector turns.

FIRST KISS AFTER DAYLIGHT

One of the most common questions that I am asked is how to differentiate between a pullback and a transition. The short answer is that you don't. Sometimes markets in deep pullbacks resume their longer-term uptrends and sometimes shallow pullbacks keep pulling back. You have to analyze each market on a case-by-case basis. Figure 9.6 illustrates an obvious pullback (a), an obvious transition (b), and a possible inflection point (c). Learning to recognize these patterns on the fly is critical to success in the markets.

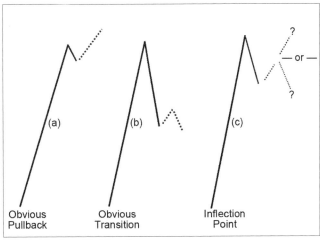

Figure 9.6 ~ Pullbacks

Markets making an obvious pullback are having what could be viewed as a normal correction. "Normal" is relative based on volatility. More volatile stocks can pull back more deeply and still be in uptrends whereas a pullback of the same magnitude in a less volatile stock could signal the end of the trend.

Markets making an obvious transition have started to implode. Ask yourself, "If this were one of my long-term holdings, would this drop have me concerned?" If the answer is yes, then those still holding the stock are probably asking themselves the same question.

The tricky part is when a market is at an inflection point. It is difficult to tell if it is just a deep pullback — one where the stock will soon resume its longer-term uptrend or, if it is actually forming a transition that could be the beginning of a major turn.

To help take the guesswork out of identifying what market phase a stock is in, a moving average can be used to gauge the strength of the possible transition. The First Kiss After Daylight defines the first thrust in the new direction by requiring daylight. The addition of the moving average makes the pattern easier to recognize. Further, although I prefer looking at as many charts as possible using very loose parameter scans, the more defined nature of the First Kiss lends itself well to more specific scans.

The pattern is very similar to Kissing MA Goodbye with the exception that it requires fewer bars of daylight and the stock must be coming off a major high or a major low.

Here are the rules for longs (Figure 9.7):

1. The stock must make a major new low. The lower the better. All-time lows make for the best setups.

2. The stock should subsequently begin to rally. During this rally, the lows of at least five bars should be above the 10-day simple moving average. Fewer than five bars is acceptable for sharp moves, especially on the short side.

3. The stock must pull back to touch the moving average. The low must be equal to or less than the moving average.

4. Enter if the trend resumes.

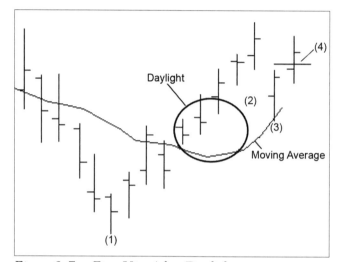

Figure 9.7 ~ First Kiss After Daylight

Now, let's look at some examples.

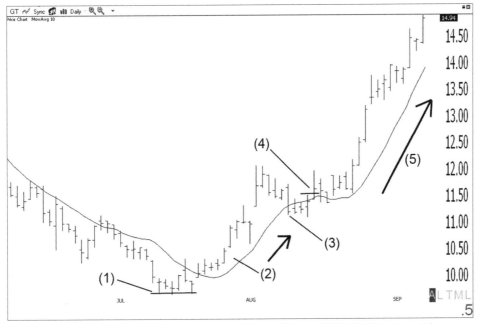

Figure 9.8 ~ GT   *Chart Created With Telechart Platinum*

1. In Figure 9.8, Goodyear Tire (GT) hits multi-year lows after a prolonged downtrend.

2. The stock begins to rally. Notice that the lows are above than the 10 day moving average. In fact, enough lows are above the moving average to also qualify this as a Kiss MA Goodbye.

3. The stock pulls back to the moving average.

4. Go long when the stock triggers by taking out the previous highs.

5. After a slow start, the stock rallies over 25 percent.

The great thing about transitional patterns is that you can occasionally catch all-time highs.

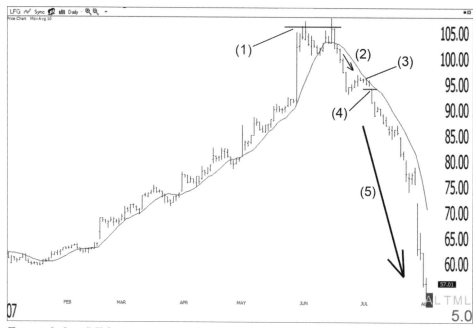

Figure 9.9 ~ LFG   *Chart Created With Telechart Platinum*

1,   In Figure 9.9, Landamerica Financial Group (LFG) makes an all-time high. Notice that this is just after a recent new high, forming a minor double top.

2.   A selloff with highs below the 10-day moving average. This action suggests that the longer term uptrend, which had many Kiss MA Goodbye patterns along the way, may be coming to an end.

3.   The stock pulls back to kiss the 10-day moving average. This also sets it up as a First Thrust pattern.

4.   The stock triggers an entry by taking out the prior lows.

5.   The stock implodes over the next few weeks. This actually turns out to be the last time the stock sees new highs. LFG subsequently files for bankruptcy.

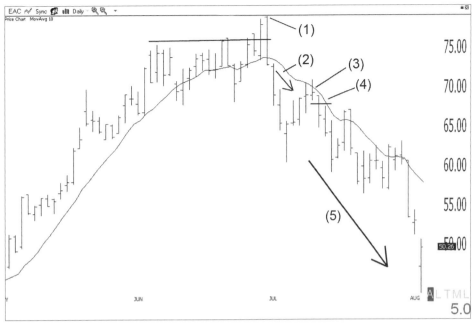

Figure 9.10 ~ EAC   *Chart Created With Telechart Platinum*

1. In Figure 9.10 Encore Acquisition (EAC) makes an all-time high. Notice that it had traded sideways for over a month. This suggested that the stock was losing momentum.

2. EAC sells off hard. The highs are below the 10-day moving average. This action suggests that the longer term uptrend may be coming to an end.

3. The stock pulls back to kiss the 10-day moving average. This also sets it stock up as a First Thrust pattern.

4. The stock triggers an entry by taking out the prior lows.

5. EAC implodes over the next few weeks.

SUMMARY
The First Kiss After Daylight is a more defined version of the First Thrust. This makes the pattern easier to recognize for the new trader. Like all transitional patterns, the advantage is that you are getting on a new trend as early as possible. Although getting in a trend early is risky, the rewards can be tremendous. Again, there is a chance you will catch the next great bull market or be short as the bubble bursts.

PATTERN APPLICATION
The pattern application is the same as the First Thrust. It works well on both the long and short sides of the market. However, since they slide faster than they glide, I tend to like the short side even more.

Ideally, the market and sector should also be making a sharp transition in trend. However, occasionally, early leaders can emerge with this pattern. By watching for a First Kiss there is a chance that you can catch a major market trend long before the masses. One final point, stocks making very sharp transitions in trend might only pull back briefly before resuming their new trend. There is a chance they will not correct all the way back to their moving average before resuming their uptrend. Therefore, as you gain experience with transitional patterns, you should look for First Thrusts first.

BOWTIES

Bowties were originally published in *Dave Landry on Swing Trading* and later in *Dave Landry's 10 Best Swing Trading Patterns and Strategies*. They have struck a chord with a variety of traders from the nimble day traders to the patient longer-term investors. They have become my most popular pattern, so I thought it was important to include them in this book.

I originally began to re-write the introduction for Bowties. However, the more I read the chapter, the more I realized that I could not say it better. Therefore, below is the introduction from *Dave Landry's 10 Best Swing Trading Patterns and Strategies*.

My style of swing trading is momentum based. Therefore, in order for me to get excited about a setup, the stock must first trend strongly in the intended direction of the trade. Requiring such strong momentum has helped to keep me on the right side of the market. However, I found that it often kept me out of stocks that were in the early phases of developing new trends. These stocks would make gradual changes (i.e., a distribution phase) and then would accelerate as the new trend emerged. I knew I had to come up with a pattern for these more gradual transitions or be willing to let them go.

Through the use of multiple moving averages, I discovered that they would often come together and spread out in the opposite direction as the market was making a major transition. That is, they would go from proper downtrend order — the faster moving averages (shorter periods) below the slower moving averages (longer periods) — to proper uptrend order — the faster moving averages above the slower moving averages (Figure 9.11).

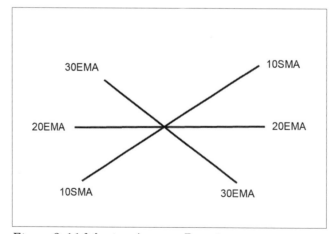

Figure 9.11 Moving Average Bowtie

When this happens over a short period of time, it gives the appearance of a Bowtie. After the Bowtie forms, it suggests that the market has made a major trend shift. However, It is still prone to correct. Therefore, you seek to enter after a minor correction.

For this pattern, I use a 10-day simple moving average, a 20-day exponential moving average, and a 30-day exponential moving average. I like the 10-day moving average because it gives me a true average price of the stock for the past two weeks (10 trading days). For longer-term moving averages, I prefer exponential moving averages since they front weight the data. Therefore, although they take into consideration the longer-term trend, they are faster to catch up with price, since more credence is given to more current data. Do not worry about the math. Moving averages are available in the even the most basic charting packages

Here are the rules for longs using 10-period simple, 20-period exponential, and 30-period exponential moving averages (Figure 9.12):

1. The moving averages should converge and spread out again, shifting from proper downtrend order (10-SMA < 20-EMA < 30-EMA) to proper uptrend order (10-SMA > 20-EMA > 30-EMA). This should happen over a period of three to four days. This creates the appearance of a Bowtie in the averages.

2. The market must make a lower low and a lower high. In other words, at least a one-bar pullback. Note, in some cases, like the First Thrust, stocks that only make a lower high (vs. a lower low and a lower high) may be considered. This is especially true when previous day is a wide-range bar.

3. Once qualifications for (2) have been met, go long above the high of (2).

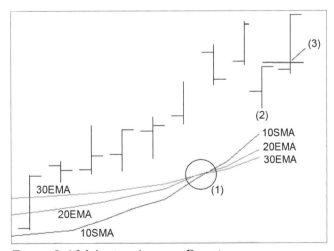

Figure 9.12 Moving Average Bowtie

With just a little experience, you will find Bowties very easy to recognize. Paying attention to the Bowtie moving averages in the indices will help keep you on the right side of the market.

Let's look at some examples:

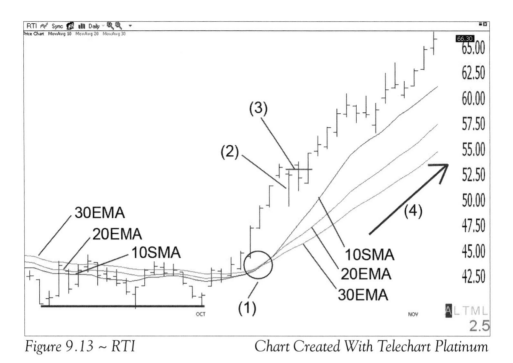

Figure 9.13 ~ RTI   *Chart Created With Telechart Platinum*

1. In Figure 9.13, after a longer-term downtrend, RTI International (RTI) begins to trade sideways. The Bowtie moving averages converge and expand, going from downtrend proper order (10SMA < 20EMA < 30EMA) to uptrend proper order (10SMA > 20EMA > 30EMA). This gives them the appearance of a Bowtie.

2. The stock makes a lower low and a lower high — a one-day pullback. This also sets the stock up as a First Thrust.

3. Go long when the stock trades above (2).

4. The stock rallies over 25 percent over the next 6-weeks and another 20 percent over the following month (not shown).

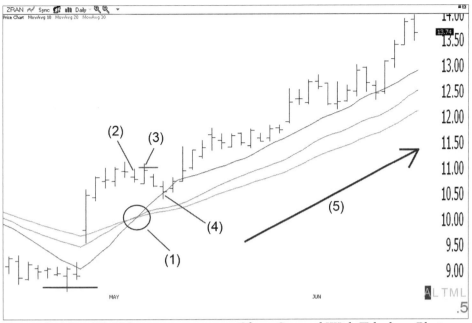

Figure 9.14 ~ ZRAN   *Chart Created With Telechart Platinum*

1. In Figure 9.14, the averages quickly converge and expand from downtrend proper order (10SMA<20EMA<30EMA) to uptrend proper order (10SMA > 20EMA > 30EMA) on Zoran Corp (ZRAN) . This gives them the appearance of a Bowtie.

2. The stock makes a lower low and a lower high — a one-day pullback. This also sets the stock up as a First Thrust.

3. Go long when the stock trades above (2).

4. The stock pulls back to kiss the moving average goodbye. Since the stock is recently reversed after hitting four-year lows, this also sets the stock up as a First Kiss after Daylight.

5. The stock rallies over 25 percent over the next six-weeks.

In spite of the hype of oil going to "$200 a barrel," oil stocks began stalling out and forming transitional patterns.

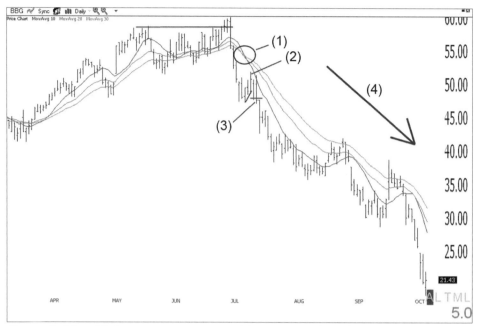

Figure 9.15 ~ BBG   *Chart Created With Telechart Platinum*

1. In Figure 9.15, Bill Barret (BBG) trades mostly sideways after rallying to all time highs. An attempt at new highs preceeds a selloff. This causes the averages to go from uptrend proper order (10SMA > 20EMA > 30EMA) to downtrend proper order (10SMA < 20EMA < 30EMA). This gives them the appearance of a Bowtie.

2. The stock pulls back for two days. Those with a good eye notice a First Thrust trigger.

3. Entry as the trend resumes.

4. The stock loses over half of its value over the next few months.

Bowties have become very popular with the daytraders. Although I preach against daytrading, I did want to show that my patterns are fractal. What works in one time frame works in others. Here is an intra-day example in the S&P 500 (Figure 9.16).

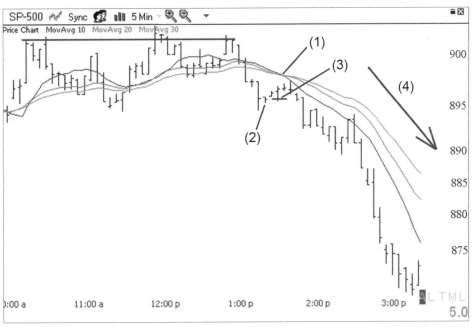

Figure 9.16 ~ S&P 500   *Chart Created With Telechart Platinum*

1. On December 11, 2008 the moving averages converge and then spread out, going from uptrend proper order to downtrend proper order on the 5-minute chart. This gives them the appearance of a Bowtie. Also notice that the S&P had traded mostly sideways prior to the Bowtie. This action suggested that the uptrend was possibly coming to an end.

2. The index begins to pull back.

3. An entry is triggered when the S&P trades below the prior low. A less aggressive entry would be to wait for additional downside confirmation. The Index pulls back to also form a First Kiss After Daylight.

4. The S&P sells off hard over the next few hours.

Through the use of multiple moving averages, Bowties often catch gradual changes in trends early. Because they are visually easy to recognize, they are a great pattern for those new to trading transitions. Further, paying attention to the proper order of the Bowtie moving averages will help to keep you on the right side of the market.

SUMMARY

Trying to pick market tops or bottoms is a loser's game. You're much better off waiting for the market to show signs that the trend is turning and then look to enter after the first minor correction. The First Thrusts, Bowties, and First Kiss After Daylight patterns allow you do just that.

Trading transitions is risky because you are fighting would could turn out to be just a correction in a longer-term trend. However, the chance of getting into a major new trend early makes them worth the risk.

PATTERN APPLICATION

The pattern application is the same as the rest of my transitional setups. Bowties work well on both the long and short sides of the market. Since selloffs typically accelerate so much faster than moves to the upside, I like the short side better than the long.

Ideally, the market and sector should also be forming Bowties. However, like the other transition setups, early leaders can emerge. By watching for Bowties in stocks, there is a chance that you can catch a major market trend long before the masses. My favorite setups occur after major lows (for longs) or after major highs (for shorts). This helps to ensure that a large number of traders are trapped on the wrong side of the market. Their exiting will help to propel the stock as the new trend emerges.

CHAPTER 10
More Stuff
You Need To Know

FLATTENING THE DEAD HORSE ON MICROMANAGEMENT

BEING MICROMANAGED AS A CONSTANT REMINDER TO NOT MICROMANAGE
Shortly after we were married, Marcy and I were getting ready to go out for dinner. I do not remember why but for some reason we were running a little late so we were scrambling to get out of the house. She was busy working on her makeup and I was getting ready to jump in the bath. And, I sort of did just that. I plopped down without bothering to check the water temperature. I immediately leaped straight up and screamed, damn that water's hot! While looking at my butt cheeks trying to determine if I had first or second degree burns as they turned from pink to bright red, I heard Marcy say, "Add some cold water to the tub." Really? You mean all these years I have been burning my butt in a hot bath and all I had to do was add a little cold water? Thank you! I am so glad we got married. We both had a good laugh. At this point, I realized that Marcy's a bit of a micromanager (and she realized that I was a bit of a smartass but I digress). I usually do not mind her micromanagement since it adds to her charm. Admittedly since I am little disorganized, I can use a little here and there.

THE TRADING WORLD VERSUS THE REAL WORLD
Although micromanagement might keep you from getting your butt burned in real life, it is one of the worst things you can do when trading. Traders at the novice and intermediate level think that the professionals know exactly when to get in and exactly when to get out. They assume that the pros exit on the slightest signs of adversity and then quickly jump back in as soon as the market reverses. After all, trading is an active verb. The truth is, if you are position trading you have to give your positions time and room to work. You have to be willing to take a little heat and risk giving up some open profits.

A COMMON MISTAKE
I debated whether or not to make micromanagement a chapter in and of itself. I thought a boring book on trading could use a little comical anecdote, but I also figured that I had already mentioned it under Trader Psychology. However, I just did not feel that I put enough emphasis on how crucial it is not to micromanage. While contemplating this, I received an email on a stock that I had recommended:

"I bought on July 17…and since that time I have been in and out four times for a loss of $57.00. Had I stayed with the initial purchase, I would have a profit of $1,115.00 in my account."

Initially, I thought this was ironic, but it is really one of the more common emails that I receive. I have the luxury of working with traders on a variety of levels. I consider this an honor. Seeing many of their mistakes is a constant reminder of what not to do. From this I know that micromanagement is one of the biggest and most common problems that plagues traders. Instead of staying with winners they try to get out at the exact time they think the market will reverse. They think "That is enough profits. How much further can the position go?" What is worse is, many do not even give trades a chance to get to that point. They second guess and exit the position one or two minutes after entry.

In my trading service, in addition to suggesting where I think a stock should be entered, I also recommend an exact area to take partial profits, and an exact area to place a protective stop just in case I am wrong. However, as soon as any position has a small adverse move, invariably, I begin getting emails second guessing the position. Admittedly, their arguments to exit early are often pretty good. "The market was up 2 percent today and the stock was down, it should have rallied. Something's wrong." Or, "it can't get through this minor resistance. If it were truly a strong stock, it should blow right past that resistance." In many cases, they go beyond the charts and begin factoring in fundamentals and news. This further confuses the issue with facts. The following is my all-time favorite example of why you should not micromanage.

In Figure 10.1, notice that Neurocrine Biosciences (NBIX) sets up as a pullback in an accelerating downtrend. The stock triggers an entry and initially moves in our favor. However, four days into the trade the stock begins to rally. At this time, I received a few emails from clients letting me know that they decided to scratch the trade, exiting at breakeven (a), the same as the entry.

Figure 10.1 ~ NBIX   *Chart Created With Telechart Platinum*

The following day, the stock implodes, losing well over half of its value overnight (b). Then, over the next few weeks, it loses over half of its value again, trading down to the high single digits. This turned out to be one of the biggest winning trades of the year (Figure 10.2).

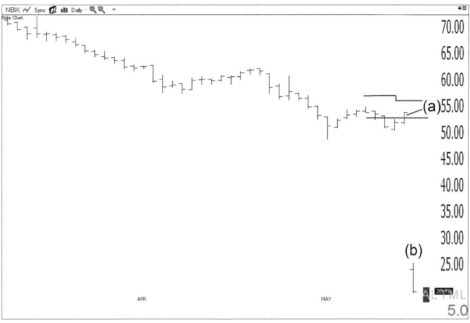

Figure 10.2 ~ NBIX   *Chart Created With Telechart Platinum*

As you can see, micromanaging yourself out of just one trade can have a huge impact on your performance.

So Why Do Traders Micromanage?

Traders are compelled to micromanage for a variety of reasons. First, the market rewards bad behavior. Second, we have a pulse, and with that pulse comes an ego with the need to be right. It also has us wired to avoid pain. Third, we live in a society that loves instant gratification. Let's explore these further.

The market often rewards bad behavior.

It seems like any time you do not exit a stock at the first signs of minor adversity, the loss becomes much bigger. And, many times if you do not take a small profit, it soon evaporates. So, micromanagement often pays over the short term but never longer term. You might get lucky and exit a dozen positions for a micro loss, but sooner or later, you are going to miss a set of trades that would have made your year.

Need for instant gratification.

In our society of fast food, microwaves, and computers, we are used to getting what we want quickly. Unfortunately, the market operates on its own time frame and it really does not care about yours. Trends take time to develop.

WE ARE WIRED TO AVOID PAIN. IT IS HUMAN NATURE.

Stocks bounce around. Yes, the trend is your friend but that does not necessarily mean that the stock will move in a straight line. There will be zigs and zags. That is one of the few things I can guarantee. Yet many still think that as a trader there must be some way to avoid all pain, that somehow you can be in and out, constantly making money while avoiding all adversity. They spend years in pursuit of a non-existent holy grail.

HOW TO AVOID MICROMANAGING

LET THE MARKET MAKE DECISIONS FOR YOU

As we have just seen, by trying to outsmart the market, you can often miss wonderful opportunities. Let the market make your decisions for you. The best thing to do is to place your orders and forget about it. If you are wrong, your protective stop will take you out. And if you are right, your trailing stop will keep you in the market for a very long time. Other than adjusting your orders, many times there is nothing to do. True, as you become more and more disciplined, there will be situations where you should exercise some discretion. However, most of the time, you do not have to do anything with open positions. This can be tough for many because trading is an active verb.

OBSESS BEFORE YOU ENTER A TRADE, NOT AFTERWARDS

Trade the best and forget the rest. Pick the best setups in the best trending stocks whose sector is also set up. Make sure many other stocks within the sector are also trending. Scrutinize each stock. Make sure all the pieces fit. Is it truly the best stock you can find? Does it have a counterpart that looks even better? After you have done your homework, place your orders and let the market prove you right or wrong. Obsess before you enter a trade, not afterwards.

PLAN YOUR TRADE AND TRADE YOUR PLAN

Know where you will enter, where you will take partial profits, where you will place your stop in case you are wrong, and how you will trail your stop if you are right. Now, follow that plan. Do not get in, change your mind and exit five minutes later.

TRADE AT A REASONABLE SIZE

If you trade at a reasonable size then you should be able to give a position time to work. And when stopped out on a position, it should be very manageable. You should be able to shrug your shoulders and say next.

WHEN IN DOUBT, TOUGH IT OUT

As previously mentioned, every now and then you will nail it. You enter and the stock immediately takes off. Following the plan is easy. Ninety-nine percent of the rest of the time the stock will back and fill. It will give you a small gain that quickly evaporates into a small loss. This makes you think that you should either get out before the pain gets any worse or exit as soon as the stock crosses back into the plus column.

One of my biggest regrets was putting "when in doubt, get out" in my first book. Within the context of the raging bull market, that was the right thing to do. Since most stocks were moving, you were foolish to stay with any stock that was not. However, over the last decade, trends take time to develop. Stocks tend to chop around more and more before finally taking off. Give positions time to work.

Do Not Watch The Screen All Day

As mentioned in Trader Psychology, watching the screen all day for a longer-term methodology can be damaging to both your financial and psychological health. Every little tick becomes something much larger than it really is. If you find yourself constantly micromanaging yourself out of big winners, set your stops and turn off your screens.

This is not to say that you should never watch a screen. It is important to watch the open, usually the first five to fifteen minutes. This will help to keep you from entering during euphoric or panicky situations and will allow you to apply more advanced techniques. After the open, you can go about your business and casually check in or set alarms for price targets so you will only be notified if action needs to be taken.

SUMMARY

Although my trades do begin as short-term setups with a narrow time frame, never forget that the real money is in longer term trends. Many traders micromanage themselves out of great trades by getting out at the first signs of adversity or by taking miniscule profits. Micromanagement can pay over the short term by helping you to avoid a loser that would have become even bigger. It can also give you a small profit on a trade that eventually would have turned into a loss. This creates a problem by rewarding bad behavior. Longer term micromanagement does not pay. It will cause you to miss the occasional home runs which are crucial to your performance. Sticking with just one longer-term winner will make up for the amount you will save on dozens of micromanaged positions.

Advanced Trading And Money Management

With experience, you will be able to apply some discretion to enter great trades early, avoid entering in euphoric situations, survive false moves, and control damage during extremely adverse moves. You will also be able to improve upon the basic money management system.

ADVANCED TECHNIQUES

Keep in mind that discretionary techniques require you to make decisions during the heat of battle. They require discipline and experience. Observe these techniques in real time to get a feel for things before trying to act. And always, use money management to minimize risks.

EARLY ENTRIES

During ideal conditions you might look to enter a position early. Ideal means that the market, the sector, and the individual stock are all strongly trending and set up in a technical pattern.

On a Front Run entry you enter (c) before the setup actually triggers (Figure 11.1). For long side trades, this means entering on intraday strength. During these times of momentum, you want to be in the market as soon as you see signs that the prior trend is resuming. You want to enter your trade before the rest of the crowd who is waiting for more a textbook entry (b). When those waiting for a more textbook entry begin buying, they will help to propel your position higher. You are Front Running these traders.

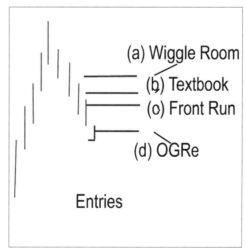

Figure 11.1 ~ Front Run Entry

The earliest entry is an Opening Gap Reversal. This is when a market opens lower but quickly finds its low and begins to rally. The best OGRe (d) entries occur when the market and sector are also forming an opening gap reversal. The advantage of this entry is that the risk-to-reward ratio can be great since markets that gap lower often quickly find their low and begin to rally. If they do not, avoid them. In many cases, the opening tick turns out to be the exact low of the day. You have to be nimble, savvy, and disciplined though. If the market turns right back down, you have to be willing to exit the trade. You have to be willing to take your lumps immediately.

Keep in mind that Front Running setups and trading OGRes are more advanced techniques and should only be used by more experienced traders under ideal conditions.

Avoiding Opening Gap And Fast Move Triggers
Emotionally charged trading often occurs around the market open. News events can flow into the market causing traders to panic into or out of positions. Unfortunately, this buying or selling often quickly exhausts itself. This action can often create an OGRe or a fast run on the market open. Let's look at how to handle these situations.

Figure 11.2 illustrates the situation in which you are looking to enter a setup (a), but the stock gaps above (b) your original entry (a). Since opening gaps can often become the exact high for the day, it is usually not a good idea to jump in with the rest of the crowd. In general, you are better off waiting a few minutes to see if the stock quickly finds its high and begins to reverse. If this occurs (c), you can look to enter if and only if the stock can trade back above its opening range. Your new entry goes above this area (d). You want to give your trade a little wiggle room just in case the stock fakes out above the open.

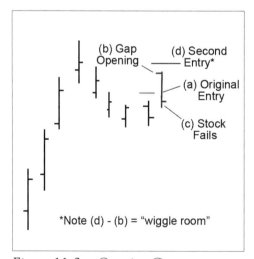

Figure 11.2 ~ Opening Gap

Referring to Figure 11.3, if the stock gaps open (b) and keeps on going (c), you are faced with a "go" or "no go" decision. This is a tough call to make. If you jump in, you risk getting caught up in the opening euphoria and could buy the high tick of the day. If you avoid the trade, then you risk missing the boat should the stock gap higher and never look back. Opening gaps that keep on going created a dammed if you do and damned if you don't situation.

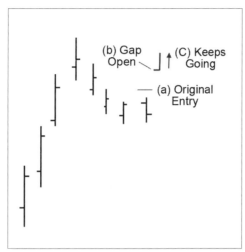

Figure 11.3 ~ Opening Gap And Go

The size of the gap can help you to make the decision. If the stock makes an extreme gap, then entering the trade is very risky. You are probably better off letting it go. Conversely, if a gap is barely above your entry, then you probably want to consider the trade since you are not buying into extreme euphoria.

TRADING FAST OPENS
Sometimes a stock will have what appears to be a fairly quiet open, but then quickly makes a fast move higher. There is a vacuum between where the stock opens and where the real market for the stock is. What appears to be a normal open for a stock could be caused by a few ignorant traders who placed orders to sell well below the real market. Market makers and pros are happy to pick these off. This delayed reaction could be also be caused by large traders waiting to see how the stock will react to a news event before jumping in. Although, the stock does not technically gap open, its behavior is very similar to a gap except that the gap occurs over a few seconds to a minute. Like a true gap, this fast buying can quickly exhaust itself. Fast opens need to be treated in a similar fashion.

Stocks often open and then immediately trade sharply higher (Figure 11.4) (a), trading through your original entry within seconds (b). In this case, you should wait to see if the stock can continue higher. If it does not and reverses, look for a new entry above the opening range (i.e. the intraday high). If the stock does continue higher (c), you are now faced with a "go" or "no go" decision. Just like the opening gap, this can create a damned if you do and damned if you don't situation.

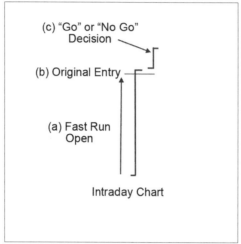

Figure 11.4 ~ Opening Range Trigger

LEARNING TO ENTER

As we have just seen, entering a trade can be little more complicated than the textbook order placed above the previous day's high. Although I have mapped out a variety of scenarios, you will need experience to learn how you will react in the heat of battle.

Those new to trading should give stocks wiggle room between the previous high and the entry. As they become more advanced, in good conditions they can use other types of entries to get them in the market sooner. In general new traders should avoid front running and trading on opening gap reversals until they gain experience. With experience, they can also use discretion to keep them out of euphoric opens.

IMPROVING MONEY AND POSITION MANAGEMENT

DAMAGE CONTROL

Sooner or later, you are going to be on the wrong side of the market. A market will gap strongly against your position. You wake up with a loss much larger than you ever intended. When this occurs, you have to keep your head while everyone else is losing theirs. Everyone wants out immediately. However, this panicky selling can quickly exhaust itself and reverse the price action. Obviously, this does not always happen. Therefore, you have to exit the stock when it does not, no questions asked.

Before we get into the details, remember that in order to implement a damage control plan, you cannot carry stops overnight. Otherwise, your stop would become a market order and you would get your order filled at the worst possible price. Now, let's break it down. Referring to Figure 11.5, your protective stop was at point (a). The stock gaps sharply against you (b). At this point, you wait to see if the stock begins to reverse. Although you may get lucky and have the opening tick become the low tick, there will often be at least some initial follow through selling on the open. You have to give the stock some additional room below the open. You have already taken the heat, a little more is not going to make a huge difference. However, you must have a point where you cannot take any more pain and you must exit if this uncle point (c) is hit. If you are fortunate enough to have the stock reverse, you can exit the stock as it rallies higher to improve your exit (d). If you are really lucky, the stock rockets higher, coming all the way to the plus column. In this case, you might actually keep the trade (e). When this occurs, you have essentially survived a knockout type move.

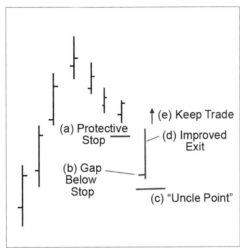

Figure 11.5 ~ Price Bar Chart

Implementing a damage control plan takes a lot of discipline. If the stock does not come back, you must exit before things get much worst. A damage control plan goes against all of the money management concepts preached in this book. You have to look at it this way, you already have a large loss on your hands, taking on additional risk is not going to make a huge difference. How much additional risk will be based on the size of the gap, the price of the stock, and the volatility of the stock. As a general rule, you probably want to give higher priced stocks (e.g. > $30) at least an additional point. On extreme gaps in volatile stocks, you might give as much as two points or more. Surviving just one major reversal will pay for the additional risks on many future damage control situations.

SURVIVING STOPS HIT NEAR THE OPEN
Sometimes a stock will open above your stop but then quickly dip below it and then promptly reverse. This can happen when your stop is very close to the market or when the overall market opens sharply lower on something like a poor economic report. Similar to damage control, you can avoid these stop hunts by waiting to see if the stock finds its low fairly quickly.

Let's break it down in Figure 11.6. The stock opens and quickly trades through our original protective stop (a). You have to be willing to exit the stock at an uncle point (b), no questions asked. If the stock does not trade through your uncle point and begins to rally, you can replace your protective stop below the intraday lows (c).

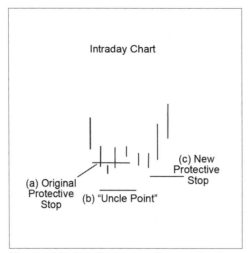

Figure 11.6 ~ Surviving Stops Hit Around The Open

Waiting to see how a stock will trade, especially in adverse conditions, can often keep you in a winning trade. Keep in mind that with any discretionary technique, it does take discipline.

SURVIVING A NICK

Sooner or later, you are going to get stopped out, often to the penny, and then watch in agony as price reverses. Let's walk through this scenario. In Figure 11.7, the stock triggers and begins to rally on the following day. You trail your stop higher (a). On day three, it sells off hard, but does not hit the stop. The stop is now very close to the market price and has the potential to get hit on the slightest amount of noise. The stock dips just enough on day four to hit the stop (b) before resuming its uptrend (c). When the stop is very close to the market like this, you can pull it to see if the market will reverse. I am talking pennies and nickels here, not suggesting that you should pull your stop and hope. If the reversal happens within cents of your original protective stop, stay with the trade. If not, then you have to exit.

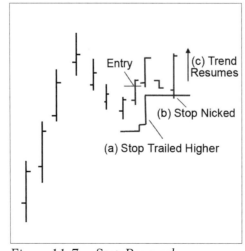

Figure 11.7 ~ Stop Reversal

GIFT HORSES

Sometimes you will enter a stock and you are instantly rewarded. In Figure 11.8, the stock has a fast move (a) over a few days to quickly approach the initial profit target (b). When this occurs, especially when the overall sector and market have also rallied sharply, it is probably a good idea to take the profit a little early. Keep in mind I am not saying take a one dollar profit when you were looking for five. I am saying if you are looking for five dollars per share, be willing to take a 4 ½ to 4 ¾ dollar profit on a fast move like this. Do not look a gift horse in the mouth since the stock has become overbought very quickly and is likely due to correct. This is especially true when the sector and overall market are also up sharply.

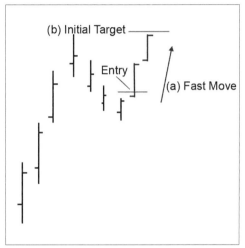

Figure 11.8 ~ Take Profits On Overbought Stocks

DO NOT SPLIT HAIRS

Sometimes a stock will rally intraday and come very close to the profit target, but it just cannot seem to get above it (figure 11.9). When this occurs, it is a good idea to not split hairs and be willing to take partial profits a little early. This is especially true in less than ideal conditions, like choppy markets, or if the overall market and sector appears to be running out of steam. Again, we are not talking taking a small profit relative to the initial profit target. Rather, we are taking partial profits as the target is approached, especially if it appears that it will not be hit.

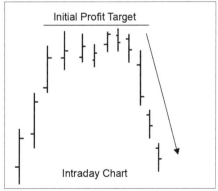

Figure 11.9 ~ Do Not Split Hairs

LET 'EM RIDE

Now here is a best case scenario. Referring to Figure 11.10, the stock makes a fast move (a) through our initial profit target (b) and keeps on going. When this occurs, you can trail a stop higher intraday (c) to capture much more than the initial profit target. On a significant rally, you might just choose to take profits while the profit taking is good. A less hands-on approach would be to place a protective stop to take partial profits at or above where you originally intended (b). If you are not stopped out, then exit half of your shares on the close. In some cases, by not watching the screen, you will be able to ride out significant intraday corrections and be pleasantly surprised by the close. Worst case, you get at least your initial profit target.

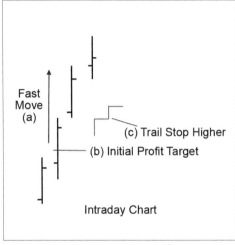

Figure 11.10 ~ Price Bar Chart

THE OCCASIONAL CASE FOR TIGHT STOPS

Many lose by thinking they are keeping risk in line with tight stops. Generally, stops must be placed outside of normal volatility. However, as you gain experience, there are certain patterns that do lend themselves to the occasional tight stop. The best case for this is when the market has corrected sharply and is due to snap back in the direction of its longer term trend. In these cases you can enter early and use a tight stop vs. waiting for an official entry and using a stop placed outside of the normal volatility. Essentially, you are taking a stab at the market. If the longer-term trend does not resume you are stopped out with a very small loss. And, if it does, the risk to reward can be quite large. The best patterns for early entries and tight stops are Opening Gap Reversals in a deep pullback or a false "V" reversal such as a Witch Hat (see *Dave Landry's 10 Best Patterns and Strategies*).

AN ALTERNATIVE INVESTMENT AS AN ALTERNATIVE TO SHORTING

On stocks that are difficult to borrow, deep in the money put options can be used in lieu of outright shorting. Another advantage of options versus outright shorting is that your risks are limited to the cost of the options in the event of a catastrophic adverse move. They can also give you staying power during vicious covering rallies. They are not without their disadvantages. Options are a complex derivative investment. It is, however, beyond the scope of this book to cover options. For more details on using options as a substitution for stock, see *Dave Landry on Swing Trading*.

SUMMARY

With a little experience, you will be able to apply some advanced discretionary techniques to greatly enhance your trading. This is provided of course that you are willing to be disciplined and are following proper money management.

Putting The Pieces Together

Omnivision Technologies (OVTI) sets up as a *Kiss MA Goodbye* (Figure 12.1). The stock is also coming off of major lows and recently set up as a *Bowtie (not shown)*.

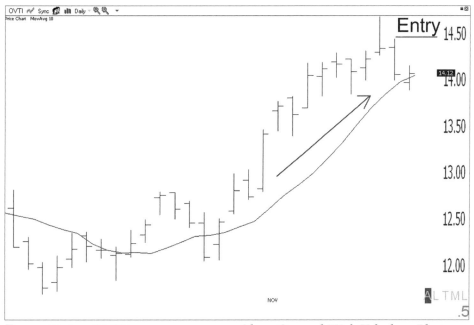

Figure 12.1 ~ OVTI   *Chart Created With Telechart Platinum*

Since the current bar is a fairly narrow range bar, a good entry would be above the prior day's high of 14.50. Before we consider this trade, we must check the sector and market action to make sure they are also in uptrends.

The Semiconductor-Integrated Circuits are in an uptrend (Figure 12.2).

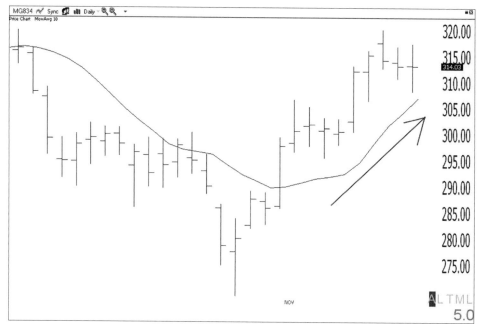

Figure 12.2 ~ SOX　　　　　*Chart Created With Telechart Platinum*

The overall market, basis the S&P 500 is in an uptrend (Figure 12.3).

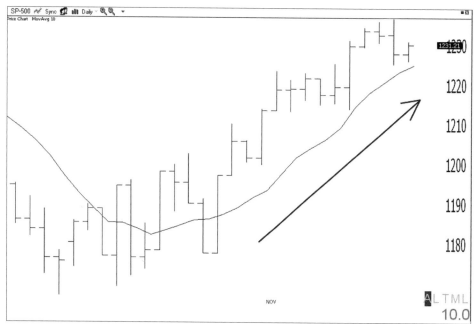

Figure 12.3 ~ S&P 500　　　　　*Chart Created With Telechart Platinum*

Since OVTI is a technology stock, we better also verify that the Nasdaq, which better represents technology stocks, is also in an uptrend (Figure 12.4).

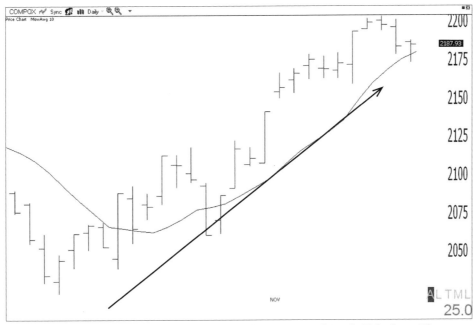

Figure 12.4 ~ COMPX   *Chart Created With Telechart Platinum*

Now that we have the three pieces of market, sector and stock in place, we can look to enter the trade. Before we do, we need to determine how many shares to trade. To do this, we must first determine where a reasonable protective stop should be placed. Eyeballing the chart in Figure 12.1, we see that the stock has had a range of around ¾ of a point lately. Further, it has recently shown that it can move a point or so over a few days. We decide that we will risk 1 ½ dollars. Again, there is no exact place to put the stop. Looser stops will help keep you in the position should the trend resume but losses will be larger if it does not. Tighter stops help mitigate large losses but may be hit on noise alone.

We now must determine how many shares to trade. We decided that we will risk no more than 1 percent of our $100,000 trading account. This way, barring overnight gaps, the worst we can do is lose $1,000 on the trade. We divide our amount risked by points risked to determine the number of shares ($1,000 risked / 1.5 points = 666.67 shares). Since we do not want to trade an odd number of shares, we decide to round down to 600 shares. This keeps our risk slightly below 1 percent/$1,000 (600 shares * 1.5 points = $900/.9 percent) should we get stopped out.

We previously determined that our entry will be at $14.50. Using $1.50 as a protective stop, we will place our protective stop at $13.00 ($14.50 – $1.50 = $13.00) if triggered. We then add the distance from the entry to our protective stop (1 ½ points) to the entry to give us a profit target of $16.00 ($14.50 + $1.50 = $16.00). We will also use the $1.50 risk parameter for our trailing stop should the stock move in our favor.

Now that we have done all of our planning, we know exactly where we will enter ($14.50), how many shares we will buy (600), where we will place our protective stop ($13.00), where we will take partial profits ($16.00), and how we will trail our stops ($1.50 below the closing price).

In Figure 12.5, OVTI triggers an entry (a) at $14.50. We buy 600 shares and immediately place a protective stop at $13.00 (b). The stock rallies nicely, closing the day at $14.99 — so far, so good. We then trail our protective stop higher (c).

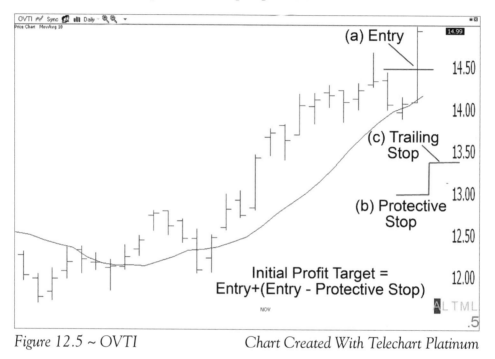

Figure 12.5 ~ OVTI   *Chart Created With Telechart Platinum*

We are trailing at 1½ points, the same as the distance from the entry to the original protective stop. Therefore, we subtract $1.50 from $14.99 to give us $13.49. To make the math easy, I usually just round down to the nearest 5 or 10 cents. This also gives me a little more wiggle room on the stop and makes it easier to remember where the stop is. For now, we will keep it more precise. However, in actual trading I prefer to round the numbers down.

In Figure 12.6, we see that the stock gaps nicely higher and continues higher to hit our initial profit target (d) of $16.00. We exit half of our shares for a profit of $450 ($16.00 – $14.50 = 1.5 * 300 = $450.00) and immediately move our stop to breakeven (e), the same as the entry (a). Now, barring overnight adverse gaps, the worst we can do is breakeven on the remaining shares. The stock continues higher during the day to close at $16.37, 37 cents above our initial profit target. Therefore, we continue to trail our stop higher, $1.50 (f) below the close ($16.37 - $1.50 = $14.87).

The following day the stock continues higher. We once again raise our stop (g) to $1.50 points below the close ($16.95- $1.50 = $15.45).

The next day, the stock closes flat. Therefore, there is no change in the trailing stop (h).

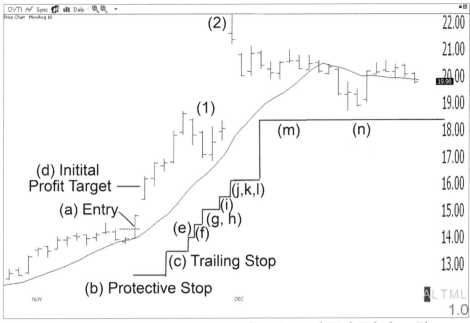

Figure 12.6 ~ OVTI   *Chart Created With Telechart Platinum*

The stock begins to accelerate higher. We have a large open profit, $18.00 – $14.50 = $3.50 or 24 percent ($3.50 * 300 = $1050.00), we can widen our trailing stop. This will help us to participate in a longer-term trend. Instead of trailing at $1.50, we now open it up to $2.00. The stock closes at $18.00, so we raise our trailing stop (i) to $16.00 ($18.00 - $2.00 = $16.00).

The stock gains another 80 cents to close at $18.80. We then increase our trailing stop (j) to $2.00 below that level ($18.80 - $2.00 = $16.80).

The stock drops over the next two days (1) therefore, the trailing stop remains the same (k). Then, the stock begins to rally. However, since it does not close at a new high, the trailing stop still remains the same (l).

OVTI then skyrockets and closes over $3.00 or 18 percent higher (2). On a windfall like this, there are two things to consider. One, you might want to exit some additional shares while there is so much euphoria over the stock. Two, you are now in a position where you can trail your stop more loosely on your remaining shares to hopefully continue to participate in a longer-term trend. Therefore, we open up our $2.00 stop to $3.00 (m) below the closing price ($21.56 – $3.00 = $18.56). After all, it gained more than this today alone.

OVTI then begins to trade sideways over the next month or so. Since it does not make a new closing high during this period, the trailing stop remains the same (n).

Notice in Figure 12.7 that the stock begins to rally, but we do not adjust the stop higher until the stock closes at a new high. The stock then breaks out (1). Therefore, we once again trail the stop higher, $3.00 below the closing price (o). In a case like this, since we have a nearly 60 percent profit, I would round down and trail the stop at $20.00 versus $20.16 ($23.16 – $3.00 = $20.16). On another note, if you look carefully, you will see that the stock closed a few cents above the previous closing high the day before it broke out decisively (2). I would not bother adjusting the trailing stop higher. My point is that as profits grow, you can become more and more liberal with your trailing protective stop since you are playing with the market's money.

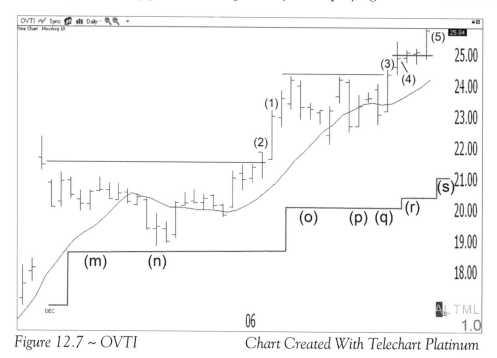

Figure 12.7 ~ OVTI   *Chart Created With Telechart Platinum*

Since the stock continues to rally, we decide to give it even more room to breathe. We loosen our trailing stop to $4.00 below the closing price (p). We do not have to do anything to open the stop up. We just leave it where it was two days prior (o).

The stock closes only 2 cents above the prior highest close (3) so we do not bother raising the stop higher. OVTI again closes at a new high, but it is only 18 cents above the prior closing high. Therefore, we just leave the trailing stop the same level (q). As you see, by doing nothing as the stock climbed higher, our stop has now opened up to $4.50 below the close.

OVTI breaks out to new highs (4), closing at $25.04. Since we are trailing at $4.50 points, we ratchet the stop up to $20.50 (r). As we have over a 72 percent profit, we are not going to worry about the extra 4 cents.

The stock once again closes at marginal new highs. Since we have a huge open profit, we are not going to bother to with a few nickels. By doing nothing, we have effectively loosened our stop to $4.73. The stock breaks out and closes at new highs (5). We then trail our stop higher. Again, since our open profits are so large, we can keep it simple and just raise our stop to $21.00 (s). We now have nearly a $5.00 trailing stop.

In Figure 12.8, the stock trades sideways over the next few days so no new action is required. It then makes a new closing high but only by a few cents (1). We do not bother with the trailing stop. The following day, the stock breaks out to close at a new high at $27.09 (2). We bump the stop up to $22.00 (t), trailing it at a little more than a $5.00 stop.

OVTI trades sideways for over two weeks. It makes a very marginal new closing high (3) but again, we leave our stop the same. The stock then has a serious correction but having a loose stop allows us to ride out this adverse move. The stock begins working its way higher but we do not adjust our trailing stop higher until it makes a significant new closing high — and it does. Keeping with the round number concept, we then raise our trailing stop to $24.00. This puts our trailing stop at nearly $5.50 below the closing price (u).

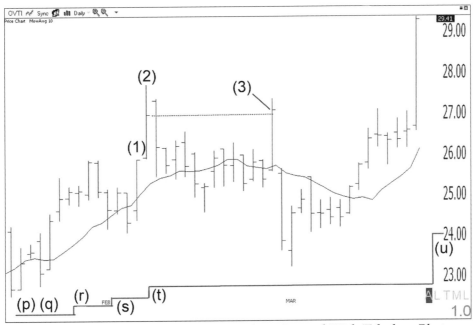

Figure 12.8 ~ OVTI   *Chart Created With Telechart Platinum*

After a one-day pause, the stock closes higher for three consecutive days (Figure 12.9). We trail our stop higher (u,v). We are now right at $5.71 below the close. The thinking now is to "open up the stop" to $6.00 by simply doing nothing.

OVTI trades sideways so the trailing stop is unchanged. It does make a marginal new closing high (1) but we do not bother raising the stop. Then, a breakout decisively to new highs (2). We now trail our stop $6.00 below the close (w). The stock continues to rally, closing at new high of $33.87. To keep it simple, we trail our stop $6.00 below this level, round numbers, to $27.50 (x). The stock makes a marginal new high (3) but we once again do not bother splitting hairs.

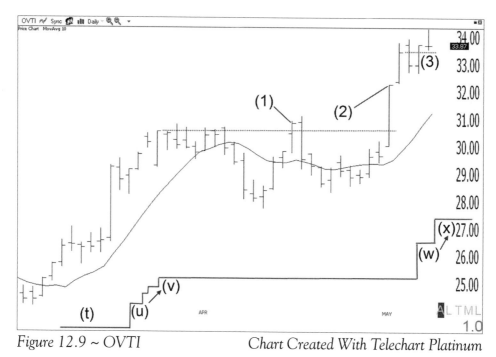

Figure 12.9 ~ OVTI   *Chart Created With Telechart Platinum*

As you can see in Figure 12.10, OVTI implodes over the next few days and takes our trailing stop. This gives us a profit of $13.00 per share ($27.50 – $14.50 = $13.00), or $3,900 on our remaining shares, bringing the total profits to $4,350. This is great when you consider that the initial risk was only $900.

Although $6.00 plus might seem like a lot to give up, keep in mind that stocks in strong trends often correct deeply before resuming their trend. You have to focus on what you have accomplished and not what you gave up. In this case, you caught a 90 percent gain in a stock. Provided you keep risks in line on the losing trades, it only takes a few of these big winners each year to have a good year.

Figure 12.10 ~ OVTI   *Chart Created With Telechart Platinum*

Remember, in trading there are always trade offs. Looser stops help to keep you in a trade should it become the mother off all trends. However, obviously you will give up a considerable amount if it does not.

Now let's review the entire trade. We played it close to the vest when the trade started (Figure 12.5) and then opened things up as the stock proved itself (Figures 12.6 thru 12.9). Notice that what started as a short-term trade using shorter-term money management and position management became a longer-term winner applying longer-term position and money management.

Referring to Figure 12.10, let's look at what became of OVTI after our stop got us out of the trade. Notice that the stock continued to slide and made a round trip all the way back to where we initially entered. Without money management, this nearly 100 percent gain would actually have resulted in a losing trade. This is yet another testament on why you should trade, not buy and hope.

You may have noticed that the example I used was a little dated. Since most do not short stocks, I Figured that I should use an example of buying a stock. However, since we have been in a bear market for so long, I had to go back a couple of years in my trading records and charts for this and many other long examples in this book.

POST MORTUM

Since this chapter was written, the market has rallied significantly (as of Spring 2010). This has provided us with numerous opportunities. Therefore, see my website and online webinars for more up-to-date examples.

SUMMARY

A trade begins with a short-term pattern that appears to have both short-term and longer-term potential. Market and sector confirmation help to stack the odds in our favor. We risk a small amount, usually 1-2% of the portfolio if stopped out. The trade is managed like a short-term trade until it proves itself. We then become more liberal with our trailing stop to position ourselves to ride out a longer-term winner. As you can see, money and position management is crucial for your success. Big winners can occasionally be captured in stocks that would have resulted in losses by simply buying and holding.

CHAPTER 13
Closing Thoughts

Stocks don't always go up over the long run. Buying low is a loser's game. Many stocks that seemed low in 2008 declared bankruptcy in 2009 and 2010. There are no good companies.

Even well diversified General Electric (GE) lost 70 percent of its value in the 2008-2009 bear market. Often there is no reasoning for why a stock or market goes up or down. Stocks do not trade on reality. Stocks trade on the perception of reality. This perception is based purely on the emotion of market participants. We can read their psychology through technical analysis, and only through technical analysis. Charts, and only charts, show what stocks have done, and what they will likely do next. Technical analysis doesn't have to be that technical. Simply drawing arrows on your chart to determine the direction of the trend will keep you on the right side of the market.

TRADE THE BEST AND LEAVE THE REST
I put a tremendous amount of time into finding the best examples for this book. I searched through years of my trading records, stocks that I had recommended, and thousands of historical charts. I also paid careful attention to every current chart to see if it would turn into a great example for this book. Although I harped on money management to temper your expectations and show that losses are a part of trading, the examples are well chosen.

After searching through a few thousand charts and only coming up with a handful of examples, I found myself beginning to feel a little guilty. In spite of all my preaching about money management, I began to wonder if I am giving my readers unrealistic expectations. Is this really fair? At that point it hit me. Although I consider myself very selective, seeing these obvious fantastic setups made me realize that I should be even more selective. I told myself that I should only trade stocks that look like the ones I put in this book. And, you should too. Besides looking at hundreds of trades and thousands of charts, I also read through thousands of emails to make sure I covered all topics. Like my previous books, I have worked hard to put everything you will need into this book. Although I think I did a great job, you are still going to need some experience before diving in.

START SMALL AND BUILD

Study historical charts. Look for trends, transitions, and my setups. Study what worked, and more importantly, what didn't. Mimic my nightly analysis. Look at thousands of charts daily. Initially, it might seem like a lot work. With time though, you will get better and better. You will soon have a great feel for what the market will likely do next.

Begin paper trading. Assuming you've done your homework, I am willing to bet that you will soon become a successful paper trader. As I said in Trader Psychology, I have yet to meet an unsuccessful paper trader.

Begin actual trading. Trade at a size that is so small, that it's meaningless. It is a lot easier to do the right thing when the mortgage isn't on the line. Once you have made the transition from successful paper trading to real dollars, slowly increase your size. You eventually want to approach the one to two percent per trade figures.

A simple approach to the market can work quite well, but I never said it was easy. Knowing what should be done is not difficult. Actually doing it is very hard. You have to be able to follow your plan while keeping your emotions in check. You cannot control the market. The only thing you can control is you. Never forget that money management will cure a multitude of sins. Start small and build. And always remember: Trade the best and leave the rest!